Library of
Davidson College

Qian Zhongshu

Twayne's World Authors Series

William Schultz, Editor of Chinese Literature
The University of Arizona

TWAS 660

Qian Zhongshu

By Theodore Huters

University of Minnesota

Twayne Publishers • *Boston*

Qian Zhongshu

Theodore Huters

Copyright © 1982 by G. K. Hall & Company
Published by Twayne Publishers
A Division of G. K. Hall & Company
70 Lincoln Street
Boston, Massachusetts 02111

Book production by John Amburg

Book design by Barbara Anderson

Printed on permanent/durable acid-free
paper and bound in The United States
of America.

Library of Congress Cataloging in Publication Data

Huters, Theodore.
  Qian Zhongshu.

  (Twayne's world authors series; TWAS 660)
  Bibliography: p. 177
  Includes index.
  1. Ch'ien, Chung-shu,, 1910-   —Criticism and
interpretation. I. Title. II. Series.
PL2749.C8Z69   895.1'8509   82-888
ISBN 0-8057-6503-4   AACR2

To my parents

Contents

About the Author
Preface
Chronology

> *Chapter One*
> Life and Times   *1*
>
> *Chapter Two*
> The Shorter Criticism   *13*
>
> *Chapter Three*
> Tan Yi Lu   *37*
>
> *Chapter Four*
> The Essays   *70*
>
> *Chapter Five*
> The Stories   *96*
>
> *Chapter Six*
> Fortress Besieged   *118*
>
> *Chapter Seven*
> A Short Evaluation   *155*

Notes and References   *158*
Selected Bibliography   *177*
Index   *183*

About the Author

Theodore Huters received the Ph.D. from Stanford University in 1977 and taught for the next four years at the University of British Columbia. He is currently a member of the Department of East Asian Studies at the University of Minnesota, where he teaches Chinese language and literature. He is coeditor of the anthology *Revolutionary Literature in China*.

Preface

Qian Zhongshu sums up many of the paradoxes of modern Chinese letters. Determined to hold himself aloof from political involvement, he has nonetheless been subject to the maelstrom of political events that make up the history of China over the past fifty years. He has been a writer committed to the separation of literature from biographical determinism, yet the life of the protagonist of his greatest work of fiction bears a singular resemblance to his own. As a literary critic intent upon the transmission of traditional Chinese culture, he has been steadfast in casting a cold eye upon some parts of that culture that conventionally were held in high regard, and he has never lost the opportunity to apply insights to his study of the tradition gleaned from his extensive knowledge of Western aesthetics. And as someone who views life as tragedy, he has a particular disposition to make people laugh. Anyone lacking Qian's diverse brilliance would probably have foundered on this series of seeming contradictions, but it is perhaps precisely this ability to combine such heterogeneous attributes that accounts for the persistent fascination he holds for Chinese intellectuals.

In terms of genre alone, Qian has produced noteworthy work of greater variety than anyone else in modern China. His criticism demonstrates a phenomenal control over the entire corpus of traditional literature as well as a knowledge of European literatures that would put many Western scholars to shame. He is also a master stylist in the three quite different linguistic media of English, literary and modern Chinese. His novel *Wei Cheng* [Fortress Besieged] is regarded by many to be the crowning achievement of modern Chinese literature. C. T. Hsia did not overstate the case when he bestowed Qian with the distinction of being "[China's] leading man of letters of our age."[1]

QIAN ZHONGSHU

It must always be humbling to write a book on a living author: he or she is, as it were, constantly at one's shoulder, able to gainsay even the most precious insights. The problems are compounded when the subject is as formidable a literatus as Qian Zhongshu. Even the fact that there are few people alive who can match his erudition provides scant comfort when I have set myself the task of taking the measure of his various achievements. I can only hope that this book does not fall too far short of the splendid standard he has set in all the literary endeavors he has undertaken.

This book is at best a partial survey of his work: the publication of what he regards as the *summa* of his career—*The Pipe-Awl Chapters*—has not reached North America at this writing. The decision on whether or not to postpone the long-promised submission of this book in order to include a chapter on that work was not easy. In the end, I decided that, judging from the fragments of *The Pipe-Awl Chapters* I have seen, it would in effect be an insult to relegate it to treatment in what would have had to be a single and rather short chapter.

Qian's breadth is reflected in the diversity of genres discussed in this book. Following a brief discussion of his life and some of the influences upon him in Chapter 1, Chapters 2 and 3 go on to treat his literary criticism; Chapter 3 is devoted solely to *Tan Yi Lu,* Qian's protean analysis of the Chinese literary tradition completed in the 1940s. Chapter 4 examines Qian's familiar essays of the late 1930s in some detail, focusing on their formal relationship to his later narrative work. That narrative work, in turn, is the subject of Chapters 5 and 6, the former dealing with his short stories and the latter with his one novel, *Fortress Besieged.* I have attempted to show in each of the chapters how Qian copes with that exceedingly knotty, or even, for most modern Chinese authors, insoluble problem of balancing the weight of Chinese tradition with the demands of a pressing social and literary modernization.

The chapter on *Tan Yi Lu* in particular has benefited from the advice of two exceptional advisors, Professors James J. Y. Liu and Chia-Ying Yeh Chao. The errors that remain are my responsibility. The people who granted me interviews to discuss Qian's

Preface

life include Professors Luo Xianglin, Stephen Soong (Song Qi), Wang Zuoliang, and George K. C. Yeh (Ye Gongchao), and I thank them all. The person who provided me with the most information on the theretofore mysterious subject of Qian's life was Mr. Qian himself, and I am particularly grateful to him for the time he so graciously spent with me at the end of what must have been an exhausting and often tiresome tour of American university campuses.

Most of all I should like to thank my wife, Pauline Yu, without whose expert assistance on all matters this book would never have been possible.

Theodore Huters

University of Minnesota

Chronology

1910	Qian born in Wuxi, Jiangsu province.
1929	Matriculates at Qinghua University.
1932	Publishes first reviews in *Xin Yue Yuekan*.
1933	Graduates from Qinghua, takes teaching post at Guanghua University in Shanghai.
1935	Goes to Oxford on Boxer Indemnity Scholarship.
1937	Receives B. Litt. degree from Oxford. Leaves for year in Paris.
1938	Returns to Shanghai; leaves for Kunming to teach for a year at Southwest Associated University.
1939	Returns again to Shanghai; departs again for Hunan province.
1939–1941	Teaching at Lantian Normal College in Baoqing, Hunan. Begins work on *Tan Yi Lu*.
1941	Returns to Shanghai again for duration of war. *Written on the Margin of Life* published.
1941–1945	Resident in Shanghai in the French concession. Teaches at Aurora Women's College. Finishes *Tan Yi Lu* and writes *Fortress Besieged* and the stories collected in *Humans, Beasts and Ghosts*.
1946–1948	Takes position at National Jinan University. Editor of *Philobiblon*. *Humans, Beasts and Ghosts* (1946), *Fortress Besieged* (1947), and *Tan Yi Lu* (1948) published in Shanghai.
1949	Takes up post at Qinghua University in Peking.
1952	Leaves Qinghua for position as senior fellow of the Institute of Chinese Literature of the Chinese Academy of Sciences.

1958	Publishes *Annotated Anthology of Song Poetry*.
1978	Takes first trip abroad in forty years, to European sinological conference in Italy.
1979	Accompanies delegation from the Chinese Academy of Social Sciences on American tour. First two volumes of *The Pipe-Awl Chapters* published.
1980	Final two volumes of *The Pipe-Awl Chapters* published.

Chapter One
Life and Times

For all the attention that Qian Zhongshu has received in the years after the mid-1970s, very little about him was published in any language before then. In fact, owing to the confusion brought to the literary world by the civil war of 1946–49, the period when most of Qian's work was published, few of the remarkable generation of non–Communist party writers that emerged after 1945 became very well known. The general chaos in the economy and in the publishing industry in particular brought an abrupt end to the profusion of literary histories and reminiscences that provide us with such an abundance of material concerning the literary scene of the 1920s and 1930s. More than that, however, authors of the 1940s had missed the prewar age of the writer as hero and came upon the literary stage at a time when most new writers were attempting to midwife a new proletarian culture into existence. Qian, with his fiction's detailed descriptions of the urban upper crust and his criticism's evident appeal to patrician taste, was especially out of harmony with the main intellectual current of the times.

Even if complete literary memoirs for the 1940s had been written, however, it is unlikely that Qian would have figured very prominently in them. As Leo Lee has demonstrated, much of the high profile which writers assumed in the prewar years resulted from assiduous care paid to personal publicity;[1] the large number of literary coteries and factions was a manifestation of this phenomenon on a collective level. Far from being intent on participating in this scene, Qian sought as much as possible to avoid it and remain a private person (recently, he even described himself as "antisocial").[2] As one can see from his fiction, he did more than avoid the literary wars; he clearly held the majority of the new literati in quiet contempt. Qian's success at avoiding attention is perhaps best measured by the admission of that chronic recorder of the literary stage—Zhao Jingshen—that he had not heard Qian's name until 1943, a full ten years after Qian had published a remarkably precocious series of book reviews in *Xinyue Yue Kan* [Crescent Moon Monthly].[3]

The few extant accounts of Qian's life up to 1949, such as that of his classmate Zou Wenhai,[4] prove to be deficient in factual information, which lends substance to Qian's remarks about the tendency of Chinese writers to substitute a poetical impulse for an historical one when writing about the past.[5] Fortunately, Qian's participation in a delegation to American universities sent by the Chinese Academy of Social Sciences in the spring of 1979 gave him the opportunity to set the biographical record straight.

Early Years

Qian was born on November 21, 1910, in Wuxi, a city on the Grand Canal above Suzhou and not far from Shanghai; Wuxi is in the Jiangnan region of Jiangsu province, an area traditionally regarded as the heartland of Chinese culture. His family was austere and conservative. His father, Qian Jibo, was born in 1887 (six years after the iconoclast Lu Xun), but it would be difficult to ascertain from the elder Qian's scholarship that the twentieth century had in any way impinged upon the Chinese literary tradition. The son's reticence concerning autobiography was not inherited from his father, who wrote a short account of himself and his family background in 1935 which provides a good deal of information about the Wuxi Qian's.[6]

The picture that emerges is one of strict adhesion to traditional ways of scholarship. The family, like most others of comparable status, maintained an academy to educate its children, who were inculcated there against what were seen as the trendy fancies of modernization. Schools were regarded with suspicion, and the young were enjoined to pursue learning rigorously and to avoid the pursuit of fame through the writing of beautiful essays. Qian Zhongshu's upbringing, however, differed in several crucial ways from that of his father. One of the principal variants is that—

having been born in 1910—the younger Qian was sent to school; by the 1910s, private academies were in decline and almost everyone went to school. According to Zou Wenhai, the younger Qian was, because of his abilities at literature, the darling of his teachers and the bane of his classmates: the sound of lesson recitals emanating from the Qian household led other parents to exhort their offspring to greater efforts.[7] Upon graduation from primary school, Qian went to the secondary school in Suzhou that was affiliated with Shanghai's St. John's University, finally returning to Wuxi to complete high school in 1929. C. T. Hsia quotes Qian as saying that, prior to the age of fifteen and to the great chagrin of his father, the younger Qian evinced no real commitment to classical learning.[8] Indeed, Qian confessed in an article written in 1965 to have had an omnivorous appetite for fiction, both traditional Chinese and—after his discovery of it—the foreign work translated by Lin Shu; he even credits part of his eventual decision to major in foreign languages to the desire to read Western narrative works in the original inspired by Lin Shu's translations.[9]

Whether from lack of application or of a general aptitude for mathematics, Qian placed only fiftieth out of two hundred students accepted in the 1929 entrance examination to Peiping's Qinghua University. Qian admits that his math score was not very high, but he denies the rather charming story originating with Zou Wenhai that it was a zero. A combination of talent and a certain arrogance brought him fame while an undergraduate at Qinghua; most of his contemporaries remember him clearly. Professor Luo Xianglin, two years his senior, recalls Qian as a sophomore challenging in casual conversation the scholarly acumen of Zhu Ziqing and Feng Youlan, the heads of the Chinese and philosophy departments, respectively.[10] Even more shocking to convention was Qian's averral that his own father's learning "was insufficient." Among the teachers he did respect was Wu Mi, the "new humanist" student of Harvard's Irving Babbitt. As Qian wrote in 1937 of the much maligned Wu:

Young Chinese students of my generation owe him a great deal. He first emphasized the "continuity of letters" and advocated the study of comparative literature which should include our own "old" literature within its purview. He alone of all practicing Chinese critics of a decade and a half ago has "synoptical" knowledge of European literary history.[11]

Qian impressed a number of his teachers; Wu, for instance, recommended him to fill a temporary vacancy in the foreign languages department while still a second-year student, and Ye Gongchao, editor of *Crescent Moon* as well as professor at Qinghua, published Qian's book reviews before the younger man had even graduated from college. During his time at Qinghua, Qian also published in the school magazine, *Qinghua Zhoukan* [Qinghua Weekly]. The only one of these articles that I have seen is the sort of meticulous scholarship in the traditional mode on points of less than overwhelming importance that had apparently occupied his leisure time since childhood.[12]

Upon graduation he returned to Shanghai to teach English at Guanghua University, a private institution where his father headed the Chinese department. By all reports, he was a most popular teacher. During his time at Guanghua he contributed articles in English to the weekly *China Critic,* as well as writing in Chinese for *Guofeng Banyuekan* [Airs of the States Fortnightly]. I have not seen any issues of *Airs of the States,* but it has been reported that Qian published over a hundred traditional-style poems in this journal between 1933 and 1936, as well as a long essay entitled "Zhongguo Wenxue Xiaoshi Xulun" [Prolegomena to a Short History of Chinese Literature].[13] The inaccessibility of *Airs of the States* is particularly unfortunate, for Qian published virtually none of his poetry after this period, and he is retrospectively proud that the traditional scholar Chen Yan praised his poetry (as well as wondering that Qian should have majored in foreign languages rather than Chinese).[14] It was also during this time that he married Yang Jikang, better known by her pen name Yang Jiang, whom Qian had met at Qinghua, where Yang was a graduate student in the Foreign Literatures department.

In 1935 Qian won a Boxer Indemnity scholarship to Oxford, where he enrolled at Exeter College for two years; he earned the B. Litt. degree in 1937. Qian remembers his years at Oxford as having been pleasant, albeit overcast by the necessity to complete the research on his thesis. Qian certainly shared the tastes and dispositions of the post–World War I generation of English dandies: like them his favorite novels were those of Marcel Proust, and his vernacular Chinese style is marked by the "virtuoso play with cliché" which Martin Green has identified as "a major feature of English culture in this century."[15] In addition, Qian's fiction matches that of Aldous Huxley and Evelyn Waugh in skewering prominent social figures to a point just this side of libel.

Mr. Song Qi, however, recalls an earlier version of Qian's memories of England in which Qian did not regard his career at Oxford as having been very successful. His knowledge of three or four European languages was the minimal expectation at the English university, and his encyclopedic knowledge of Chinese failed to impress tutors who were ignorant of the long tradition of Chinese letters. Qian also failed his examination in Old English on the first try, something profoundly shocking to one who had always been able to count on a photographic memory. Furthermore, there is a sense in which Qian's highly refined tastes of this period were frivolous and out of tune with the times. By 1936 the depression and the Spanish Civil War had brought about in Britain a general turn from dandyism to a more serious outlook on the world; Qian's writing did not manifest this sobering of attitude until after his return to wartime China in 1938. Nevertheless, he was successful enough to gain one of the few B. Litt. degrees awarded up to that time to a student whose native tongue was Chinese, and the university thought enough of him to offer him a readership in Chinese in 1937, an offer he turned down.

Upon completion of his degree at Oxford, the Qian's spent the 1937–38 year in France, where Yang Jiang continued her studies of French literature and Qian audited courses. As C. T. Hsia observed, the existence of this third year in Europe came as a surprise to everyone to whom Qian related it on his American tour. Prior to this, everyone who wrote on Qian assumed that he—like *Fortress Besieged*'s Fang Hongjian—had returned to China in 1937. This disparity between the two lives is a salutary admonition to those who would too readily conflate them.

The War Years and After

By the time of Qian's return in the summer of 1938, most of North China and the Jiangnan region had been in Japanese hands for periods of up to a year. Three outstanding northern Chinese universities—Peking, Qinghua, and Nankai—had amalgamated during this time and moved to the unoccupied south. Settling first in Changsha, Hunan, the new institution called itself *Xinan Lianhe Daxue* (Southwest Associated University, abbreviated as "Lian Da"—"Associated U.," or "Xinan Lianda"—"Southwest Associated U."). Soon realizing the vulnerability of Changsha, the institution removed itself even farther south to Kunming in the border province of Yunnan, where it was to remain for the remainder of the war.[16] It was to Lian Da in Kunming that Qian went to teach English in the Foreign Languages department for the year 1938-39.

Previous accounts of Qian's time in the interior have been garbled by a combination of lack of reliable sources and memory lapses on the part of people who were there. Ye Gongchao, for instance, who was head of the department at the time, related that he had no memory of Qian's having taught there, which squares neither with Qian's distinct recollection of Ye's having specifically requested permission of Qian Jibo for the younger Qian to go teach in Kunming nor with professor Wang Zuoliang's memory of Ye's having personally introduced Qian as his protégé on the first day of a special advanced English class in 1938.[17] Qian's own account of his year in Kunming having been unhappy because of Ye's jealousy of Qian's popularity with students may in some way clarify the source of the discrepancy. At any rate, Qian returned to Shanghai in the summer of 1939, only to depart again for the interior two months thereafter.

His destination this time was Lantian Normal College (Lantian Shifan Xueyuan) in Baoqing, a city in a relatively remote area of southwestern Hunan. It was here that Guanghua University, accompanied by Qian Jibo, had reconstituted itself. The younger Qian describes his trek to and tenure at Lantian as undertaken more out of a sense of filiality than of any real enthusiasm for the task itself. (It may be noted parenthetically that the Sanlü University of *Fortress Besieged* is a caricature of Lantian rather than of Associated.) It was in Baoqing that Qian began his great work of literary criticism, *Tan Yi Lu* [Discourses on Art].[18]

Yang Jiang had accompanied her husband neither to Yunnan nor to Hunan, having stayed in Shanghai to care for her parents and mother-in-law. In late 1941 Qian returned to Shanghai to attend to his very ill father-in-law and was trapped in the coastal city by the outbreak of the Pacific War and Japan's conquest of what remained of the sovereignty of the foreign concessions there. The time from 8 December 1941 until August of 1945 was difficult for all residents of Shanghai, but it was particularly arduous for prominent members of the Chinese intelligentsia, who were caught between pinched employment opportunities and Japanese-sponsored blandishments to rally to the cause of a "Greater East Asia." Like many of their cohorts, Qian and Yang Jiang spent those years in the French concession, where Vichy rule blunted somewhat the intellectual pressures of the occupation. Qian eked out a living teaching private students as well as securing an appointment at the French Catholic Aurora Women's College (Chendan Nüzi Daxue). At the same time he continued work on *Tan Yi Lu* and turned his hand for the first time to the writing of fiction. Yang Jiang for her part was writing plays that were successfully produced as part of the "theater boom" of wartime Shanghai.[19] Not only did these bring her real fame in literary circles, but they brought in real money as well.

In spite of the straitened circumstances and intermittent oppression, the war years in Shanghai witnessed an efflorescence of literary activity. Realization of the horror of war in general and of the cynicism and self-seeking on display during the final years of the War of Resistance against Japan in particular seemed to shock a new generation of authors—such as Qian, Yang Jiang, Shi Tuo, and Zhang Ailing—out of the facile optimism that characterized much of the fiction of the earlier "romantic generation" of writers; the narcissistic posing of the 1920s and 1930s was obsolete. It is no doubt this change in background that accounts for the dark pessimism permeating much of the literature of this time. It is nonetheless obvious that life during this period had its compensations: the obverse of political and social pressure was a sense of community which encouraged literary work and kept internal squabbles and the formation of factions at a minimum. Thus Qian felt sufficient joy of life to sport a cane—an apparent concession to the dandyism which he so acutely mocks in his fiction—and to give voice to a bit of playful jealousy over Yang Jiang's newfound fame.[20] With the completion of his fiction and *Tan Yi Lu* at this time, Qian's own fame awaited only their publication.

Once the war ended, publication came very quickly. The second number of the new journal *Wenyi Fuxing* [Literary Renaissance], which appeared in February 1946, contained the first installment of *Fortress Besieged*. The serialization ran for a full year, accounting for much of the journal's success (something to which Qian admits with a characteristic and disarming lack of modesty). The work was published in a single volume in May 1947 and was in its third edition by the time of the Liberation of Shanghai in May 1949. Any book which ran through more than one edition was considered to be a "bestseller," but since editions rarely comprised over 2,000 copies, sales were not spectacular by North American standards.[21] Sales were certainly not high enough so that Qian could live off their proceeds, although the book did as well as most written by such mainstream authors as Lao She and Mao Dun. Qian's collection of stories, *Ren, Shou, Gui* [Humans, Beasts and Ghosts], had been published in 1946, and *Tan Yi Lu* followed in 1948. The two years between 1946 and 1948 thus saw the appearance of the work—all completed by 1945—on which the main part of Qian's reputation rests.[22]

Critics such as C. T. Hsia have blamed Qian's relative silence since 1948 on the Communist party's rigid policies toward literature since coming to power. This accusation must, however, be balanced against the fact that Qian produced very little for publication between 1945 and 1949, a period equal in length to that during the war when he wrote half of *Tan Yi Lu,* four stories and a very long novel. While it is true that Qian began work on another novel, *Baihe Xin* [Le Coeur d'Artichaud—The Heart of the Artichoke], he had completed less than a hundred pages by the time he misplaced the manuscript in mid-1949. As *Fortress Besieged* runs to some 450 pages in its first edition, the amount completed was probably not a very significant percentage of the proposed total. In fact, Qian's postwar creative slowdown was the rule rather than the exception among both the established and the new generation of urban writers. Mao Dun, for instance, published only a few rather skimpy stories, Ba Jin's 1946 novel *Han Ye* [Cold Nights] was his last and Shi Tuo apparently wrote nothing after he finished *Jiehun* [Marriage] in 1946. The declining economic situation and its concomitant inflation combined with a sense of political frustration engendered by the ongoing civil war to make the late 1940s a disheartening period for intellectuals in general and writers in particular.[23] Of the prominent writers, only Lao She did not abate his creative activity, and he spent most of these years in the United States.

Qian's postwar career is typical of a time of widespread moonlighting among intellectuals. Although invited to teach at Qinghua, he decided to stay in Shanghai, securing a position at the National Jinan University through the intervention of his friend Liu Dajie, the Dean of Arts and Letters. Qian also periodically commuted to Nanking to edit *Philobiblon*, the English language organ of the National Central Library; he served as well as one of two Chinese members of the advisory committee on publishing and scholarships to the British Council in China. With the advent of the new government in 1949, he returned to Qinghua to take up a professorship in the Foreign Languages department. Although again offered a job at Oxford, he chose to stay in Peking because, as Allyn and Adele Rickett quote him saying, "This is my country. There's a lot going on and I'd like to stay around and do my bit."[24]

Qian had not long been in Qinghua before he abandoned teaching for good. Along with He Qifang and Yu Pingbo, he was appointed senior fellow of the Institute of Chinese Literature when it was founded as part of the Chinese Academy of Sciences in 1952. Absenting himself from university life was probably a wise move: had he remained a teacher, his pungent wit and abrasive style would inevitably have been transformed through the medium of the more enthusiastic students' notes into weapons to be used against him in political struggle. As it was, he had as little to do with politics as possible and steadfastly refused to participate in the periodic condemnations of fellow scholars. This failure to speak ill of others in public made him no enemies, and the Institute, under the protection of the powerful Zhou Yang, was generally able prior to 1966 to shield its inmates from the worst political storms. Qian's pre-1966 detachment also preserved him from the worst excesses of the Cultural Revolution. Although his work was interrupted and he was duly sent to the countryside, he did not suffer the gross abuse that more active scholars sustained.

From his rather privileged position Qian has been able to watch the activities of his fellow intellectuals with considerable ironic detachment. He is aware of their attempts to come to terms with state power, to which he maintains an attitude more than a little reminiscent of a traditional *qingliu* ("pure stream") scholar: to the extent that men of letters break ranks and betray their own caste, he blames them rather than the functionaries of state for their unfortunate circumstances. From his point of view the greatest sin is *trahison des clercs,* the betrayal of one intellectual by another. He harbors a similarly dim opinion of scholars taking up Marxism simply out of a desire to run with the herd. Based on the frequency of such behavior, Qian passes blanket judgment on his generation of the Chinese intelligentsia as being people who were afraid to be separated from the core of political activity; the high moral coloration that scholars took on during the years after 1937 never receded, and they consequently never departed from the political arena. Qian's bleak and minimal self-assessment is that he is a person who has "not been afraid to be alone": he feared neither being without political leverage nor gradually becoming estranged from once good friends as they became entangled in political intrigues. In this solitary life, however, he has not been completely alone; he and Yang Jiang are very close, and this closeness has made their lives that much easier.[25]

Only after understanding this background do some of Qian's utterances on certain subjects become clear. For instance, his apparently cold-blooded summary of the political fates of certain people as being in accord with the principle that "the treatment you get is in direct proportion to the figure you cut" is not simply the viewpoint of one speaking from a protected position—it also stems from the awareness that he has been in that minority of intellectuals content to keep a low profile. But Qian's proviso that the essence of political wisdom lies in "knowing when not to write" contains an irreducible portion of naivety. This naivety, however, is perhaps accountable to a certain final modesty: Qian is a man of such awesome abilities and knowledge that it would be difficult for even the most ardently egalitarian regime not to treat him with more care than most of his colleagues, and his sense of the ease of survival may arise from an indisposition to recognize the full uniqueness of his own case.

In 1976 C. T. Hsia published a eulogy to Qian Zhongshu in a Taipei newspaper, *Zhongguo Shibao*. But in 1978, with the change in Chinese regime after the fall of the "Gang of Four," Qian suddenly appeared as a member of the Chinese delegation to a sinological conference held in Italy. And in April 1979, Qian—along with ten other members of the Chinese Academy of Social Sciences—arrived in New York to begin their month-long American tour. This tour introduced Qian at long last to a large number of American students of Chinese literature.

For all Qian's security under the People's Republic, before 1978 it seemed that he had had little opportunity to get much work done. Aside from some editorial work, a few articles and reviews and his annotated edition of Song dynasty poetry, little had appeared under Qian's name since 1949. In 1978, however, the Hong Kong newspaper *Da Gong Bao* published a twenty-page excerpt from a new work by Qian entitled *Guanzhui Pian* [Pipe-awl Chapters] as part of its thirtieth aniversary celebration. It was soon announced in China that the *Pipe-awl Chapters* was to be published in Peking in 1979 as part of the thirtieth-anniversary celebration of the People's Republic. It is an immense work in four volumes (the last two of which did not appear until 1980), devoted to commentaries on ten of the classic works of the Chinese tradition: the *Yi Jing* [Classic of Changes], *Shi Jing* [Classic of

Poetry], *Zuo Zhuan* [Zuo Tradition], *Lun Yu* [Confucian Analects], the *Zhuangzi,* the *Liezi,* the *Shiji* [Records of the Historian], the complete pre-Tang prose, the *Wen Xuan* [Literary Anthology], and the *Taiping Guangji.* This turns out to have been the work that has occupied the better part of Qian's time over the past thirty years; it is what he wishes to be remembered by, and its range of time periods and genres covered is suitable testament to his immense erudition. It is also characteristic of his style to keep one eye on the tradition, both in his choice of subject and the commentary form in which he discusses it, and another eye on uniting the Chinese heritage with universal culture by his frequent and precise reference to Western learning. It is thus a fitting pinnacle to a career that has encompassed, as we shall see, an enduring effort to meld old and new, Chinese and Western.

Chapter Two
The Shorter Criticism

Although much of Qian Zhongshu's literary scholarship is concerned with fine points and highly technical matters, a definite interest in complex theoretical questions often underlies what appears superficially to be a rambling or even disjointed discussion. His early critical writings of the 1930s, while generally quite straightforward, also adumbrate many of the themes that recur throughout his career as literary scholar. This is especially true of his first major publications, a series of book reviews that appeared in *Xin Yue* during 1932–33, his last year at Qinghua. According to Zhao Jingshen, they caused considerable favorable comment upon their appearance.[1] Three of them will be discussed here.

The *Xin Yue* Reviews

The first of these, and perhaps the most interesting, is an ostensibly favorable critique of Zhou Zuoren's famous *Zhongguo Xin Wenxue de Yuanliu* [The Origins of the New Chinese Literature], the book that resulted from a series of lectures given at Peiping's Furen University in 1932. In the review Qian points out some of the inconsistencies in the then newly published work, while making a number of perceptive comments on the nature of premodern Chinese literature and its relationship to the cultural tradition. Qian's first point of disagreement with Zhou is over the latter's notion of "literature for literature's sake"; Qian prefers rather the idea of "literary autonomy."[2] Although Qian does not go directly into the reasons behind his distinction, they become apparent in the course of the discussion.

The main thrust of Qian's analysis is to break down Zhou's mechanical distinction between "didactic" and "expressivist" literature. Zhou had not only isolated these as the two dominant trends in literary activity, but had also posited a rigid antinomy between them, based on a strict historicist scheme. In this scheme, didactic literature was seen to dominate during those historical periods when the government was strong and able to enforce strict Confucian ideology. Expressive literature could only flourish in periods of governmental decline when ideological control slackened. Zhou regarded the three Yuan brothers (Zongdao [1560–1600], Hongdao [1568–1610], and Zhongdao [1570–1623], and the Gongan school with which they were identified, as the quintessential representatives of the expressivist tendency. The fact that they lived during the period of political chaos that marked the final years of the Ming dynasty was seen as the key factor in their ability to advocate their heterodox theories. Zhou also felt that the May Fourth "literary revolution" against a stifling Confucian orthodoxy followed in a direct line of succession from the Gongan school.

Qian's first point of departure from this hypothesis was his perception that the predecessors of the May Fourth movement could be traced back much earlier than the seventeenth century:

Pushing even farther back, those such as Han Yu (768–824) and Liu Zongyuan (773–819), in rebelling against early Tang [dynasty prose style], as well as Ouyang Xiu (1007–1072) and Mei Yaochen (1002–1060), in rebelling against the *Xikun* [an ornate style of poetry developed in the early Song dynasty in imitation of Li Shangyin (813–858)] are in the same line. Because they were dissatisfied with the affected, artificial, formalistic literature of their times, they moved toward self-expression. How can Han Yu's opposition to "plagiarizers" or Ouyang's opposition to "picking here and there" and Mr. Zhou's quotation from Yuan Zhonglang [Hongdao] not be said to have points in common?(10)

On the basis of Zhou's having failed to recognize these earlier movements, Qian accuses him, quite justly, of having treated the literature of the Tang, Song, and Yuan "too *cavalierly*" (this and other italicized English words in subsequent translations from the Chinese originally appeared in European languages in Qian's text). The only difference Qian can adduce between the movements led by Han Yu and Liu Zongyuan on the one hand and the Gongan school on the other is that the former succeeded and the latter failed in becoming the reigning literary orthodoxy. The Gongan school thus "imparts a strong sense of evanescence and moves those with a rich sense of nostalgia for the past, such as Mr. Zhou, to a feeling of its uniqueness."

At the heart of Qian's critique lies the recognition that the main hypothesis of *Origins* rests on a fundamental misconception: Zhou's admiration for the Gongan school is based more on the fact of its failure to become orthodox than on its own merits. In this light, Qian's preference for the idea of "literary autonomy" is an important part of his critique, the concept of autonomy being more insistent upon the specific particularity of art than is the more nebulous idea of "art for art's sake." The distinction becomes clear in a more detailed examination of Zhou's historical scheme. For all his declamation about the need for a separation between politics and literature, Zhou's hypothesis about the development of literature rests strictly on the vicissitudes of political history. The relationship between politics and literature is of key importance to all modern Chinese intellectuals, and Qian's argument with Zhou Zuoren on this point is but the first of his many statements on the ramifications of the problem.

Qian does admit, however, that the distinction between didactic (*wen yi zai dao* ["literature conveys the Way"]) and expressive (*shi yan zhi* ["poetry expresses intent"]) is a real one. But he does not see the two modes rising and falling in mechanical, inverse proportion to the political situation, for the matter is more complex. To Qian, the two concepts

do not seem to be entirely unrelated propositions, as Mr. Zhou and other critics assume. In traditional criticism we do not have a unified concept of "literature"; all we have are *shi* (poetry), *wen* (prose), *ci* (lyrics) and *qu* (song-poems)—these miscellaneous categories. The reason is perhaps that the Chinese are too [guilty of] *Departmentality! Shi* is *shi* and *wen* is *wen*. They have their assigned positions; each has its own regulations and tasks. The *wen* of *wen yi zai dao* is customarily used only to refer to "ancient-style" prose *(guwen)* or to [plain] prose *(sanwen)*:

it does not encompass all that we now call "literature." . . . *Dao* has an objective existence, but *shi* is something else. *Shi* is basically secondary to *guwen*, of lower *Genre*; its goal is only to express the subjective. Emotion—*yan zhi*—does not have as large a mission as *wen*. So, for the objective *wen* we cannot but convey [*zai*] it, but as for subjective emotion, one can *Control* [*chi*] it, in the sense that "Poetry is what holds one's emotions and nature [within the bounds of propriety]."[3] The bifurcation of these two attitudes is not, as far as I know, without its element of truth. In traditional criticism, however, they are parallel and not contradictory: they cannot be called two "schools." Because of this, a good many literati who advocated didacticism never failed to "give expression to their native sensibilities" when they came to write poetry. Their poetry thus completely differs from their quotidian world of words {*wen jing*}." (11–12)

Qian goes on to demonstrate his own hypothesis by observing that the poetry composed by members of the highly orthodox Qing dynasty Tongcheng school is radically different from their didactic prose. He also points out that the influence of the Gongan school on orthodox prose theory in the Qing dynasty was not restricted to dissenters such as Jin Shengtan (1610–1661) and Li Yu (1611–1680?). Qian concludes by noting that conservative literati were just as interested in folk songs as the Gongan theorists and adds, with some irony, that members of the latter group were strong advocates of the "eight-legged essay" (*bagu wen*), regarded by Zhou as the most hidebound of all forms of writing.

Qian's marshaling of these facts in large part demolishes Zhou's theory of a simple, alternating cycle between free expression and didacticism. If Zhou's purpose in the lectures was to read into the tradition a sanction for a departure from Confucian literary norms, Qian is intent upon demonstrating that this set of norms is not nearly the bugbear which the May Fourth generation took it to be. The younger man's broad acceptance of the literary tradition would, however, have been extraordinary in the iconoclastic college students of the previous decade. A certain pessimism inhering in this acceptance is manifest in the peroration to the review, in which Qian sounds, not for the last time, the theme of *plus ça change, plus ça reste la même chose:*

Mr. Zhou quotes Lu Xun's dictum, "from revolutionary literature to obedient literature"[4] and says that all "didactic" literature is obedient. This theory is problematical. Those who study literary history all know that, within a movement, to "give free expression to native sensibility," the "native sensibility" expressed almost always falls firmly into a set *Pattern*. Moreover, to advance one step farther, the reason for desiring "revolution" is that others are not willing to obey what you yourself advocate. "The revolution has not yet succeeded,"[5] so it is necessary to continue it; but when it has succeeded, then everyone is expected to obey. This is true in regard not only to literature, but to social and political revolutions as well. So, as I say, the success of a revolution in fact is the failure of revolution in theory.(14)

A bleak assessment indeed from a man of twenty-two.

The last published of this series of reviews, which appeared in the final issue of *Xin Yue* in June 1933, discusses the *Jindai Sanwen Chao* [Anthology of Modern Prose]. This volume was a collection of essays written primarily in the period of political crisis in the seventeenth century that so fascinated Chinese literary men of the 1930s. It was edited by Shen Qiwu, and the works he selected were meant to be representative of the "expressivist" style of the earlier time.

In his review, Qian amplifies his earlier discussion of the differences between various literary styles. He begins by posing the question of how such distinctions are to be made. The two genres with which he is concerned are *wen*, the formal prose that is universally regarded in the twentieth century as being highly didactic, and *xiaopin wen*, or "familiar prose," a freer variant of *wen* looked to in modern China as a model of free expression. Before setting out his own interpretation, Qian denies a formulation of Yu Pingbo's that sums up the post–May Fourth expressivist school: it is not true, says Qian, that familiar or informal prose is simply a matter of "speaking for oneself," while formal prose means "speaking for others." In other words, he does not believe that such a clear distinction can be drawn between one's own words and those of others, citing in this context the famous motto of the Qing scholar Zhang Xuecheng (1728–1801): "Your words are everyone's" *(yan gong)*.[6]

In saying this, Qian is once again concerned with breaking down a simplistic theory that is attempting to find authority for new directions in supposed countermovements of the past. Qian argues:

> To use such elements of *Subject matter* [*sic*] as *yan zhi* and *zai dao* to make *fundamental divisions* is most improper. We do not need to refute this with any theoretical argument: all we need do is look at the essays in this collection to see that there are *xiaopin* essays which are also didactic and discursive.

If, however, one cannot draw distinctions based on content or authorial attitude, what is to be used in their stead? Qian supplies his answer:

> It is obvious that the distinction between *xiaopin* and official *wen* lies not in subject matter or content but in *style* [*gediao*] or form. How different this sort of *xiaopin* style—I call it *Familiar style* [*jiachang ti*] because of its plain exposition—is from the ornamented processional of official *wen*. This has been true for some time. (2)

He goes on to trace the origins of this "familiar style" back to the time of the Six Dynasties (ca. A.D. 220–589). He finds its beginnings not in the parallel prose for which this era is best known, however, but in a style called *bi*, which he says neither avoided parallelisms and rhythmics nor made any special effort to employ them.

Qian describes *bi* in more detail as a "carefree familiar style, one just between the *Bookish* [*pian san ya*] and the *Vernacular* [*su*]. It is definitely not the post-Tang *guwen*, that pure, uncoupled prose which became the predominant current after Han Yu's archaism [*fugu*]" (3). Qian maintains that this familiar style had been forced to lead a sort of underground life thereafter, being preserved and passed down in *biji* fiction, personal letters and in some prefaces and postfaces written by otherwise orthodox writers such as Su Dongpo (1037–1101). As a concomitant of this, the familiar style was relegated to a cognitively inferior position in letters, similar to the position of poetry as described in his review of Zhou Zuoren's lectures. Thus, the familiar style became the particular province of the good natured *"dilettantes"* in which the Ming abounded. Qian concludes that "in our age, where we talk loudly of *Technocracy,* this type of person is no doubt 'extinct,' so the Ming has become a kind of 'golden age' of the past" (4). While this is hardly a raging affirmation of traditional literary values, neither is it suffused with the pessimism that sets the tone of his review of Zhou's book. More important, in his praise of the plastic, open-ended qualities of the familiar style, Qian sets up a channel through which the heritage of the past can be useful to the modern writer. In fact, by his own account, as we shall see in the next chapter, Qian modeled himself precisely on this style when he came to write his masterpiece in the literary language, *Tan Yi Lu.*

Qian's review of Cao Baohua's poetry collection, *Luori Song* [Odes to the Setting Sun], the last of the three reviews we shall discuss, is also the longest. The latter section of it is written in a tone one does not often see in Qian's work: halfway through the article, he drops his characteristic sophisticated voice and proceeds to set forth in lyrical language his hopes for a new Chinese literature. He begins the essay by advancing a number of postulates concerning poetry and poetics, all of them astute and many of which will be addressed again in more detail in *Tan Yi Lu.* He observes, for example, that the distinction between what constitutes literature and what does not is that, while the latter is "readable," the former is "re-readable." Qian criticizes the poems under review for containing obtrusive language—language not composed with any organic conception of the poem as a whole in mind, but which is merely an agglutination of precious and therefore dead images. Poetry that is really good, he says, will cause the reader to sense the merit of the poem as a whole rather than the brilliance of individual lines or images. He also affirms that all rhetorical devices have logical bases and that Cao has violated this principle and thereby created faulty similes and metaphors. Qian sees the basis of simile and metaphor as residing in the perception of the poet: if perception is sharp, "it can see things where 'the exterior differs but the heart is the same.' It can grasp points of commonality that ordinary people cannot [at first] see, but once [demonstrated they] can understand."[7] This concern with simile and metaphor presages the extensive and brilliant use of images in Qian's later creative work.

After this harsh, even mocking, criticism is executed, Qian admits that the poems, "no matter how bad, have a sort of naive, uncultivated strength," and that Cao had not "composed [merely] a lot of *cultivated triviality.*" Noting that Cao's work contains a certain "portion of *mysticism* [*shenmi zhuyi*]," something Qian claims Chinese poetry has always lacked, he goes on to outline the nature of mysticism:

Mysticism requires the nurture and cultivation of sensibility over many years: it cannot be some slapdash application of emotion. It requires a change from the Byronic attitude of resentment over heavenly fate. It seeks to reconcile through language the universe and human life. It seeks from the sacred books of the East and West the collected wisdom of the ancients—the silver and the ink-black; it searches within the ethereal magic of a dispirited *rabbi* for a passport allowing access to the mysteries of the universe. It reaches so far, so far as to espy the kingdom of heaven in the smallest flower-petal, seeing the world in the most infinitessimal grain of sand, realizing eternal life in a single instant.[8]

These words borrowed from Blake seem to have put Qian in such a magnanimous mood that he proceeds to forgive Cao his sins and to discuss the few features of the verse which augur hopefully for more successful poems in the future. Qian decides that "the setting sun" is the wrong image for the collection's title: a more appropriate one would be "the sun about to break out of a morning mist," since "the best poems of this author are those which he has yet to write. Can there be any critique better—no, more to the point—of a new poet?" (28).

Qian's high evaluation of mysticism and simultaneous assertion that Chinese poetry had theretofore lacked it seems a bit curious in light of the constant stress in traditional Chinese aesthetics on the feelings objects engender rather than on the objects themselves. The long statement on mysticism could, in fact, almost have been a paraphrase of any one of a number of Chinese works on the theory of poetry and painting. The confusion here can only be cleared up by reference to *Tan Yi Lu* (see below, pp. 65–66), in which Qian borrows from Hegelian dialectics to outline a dynamic relationship between object and feeling in which each clearly implies the other.

If Qian fails in this review to articulate clearly his dissatisfaction with premodern Chinese poetics, the intention of taking to task his own literary tradition is clear enough. If this rebuke is put in the context of his pessimism about the possibilities of any real break with the past, seen in his review of Zhou's lectures, he would seem to be painting a rather grim picture of the possibilities for modern Chinese literature. At the same time, however, Qian's sense of the Chinese tradition as a living entity that is apparent in his review of Shen Qiwu's prose collection must be set against this bleakness. In fact, this contrast between the need for Chinese literature to break new ground, already pioneered in the West, with a concomitant dissatisfaction and pessimism toward the old, and the complaisance toward and sense of continuity with the tradition remains a pervasive ambivalence in all of Qian's writings.

Some Hard Looks at the Tradition

His negative attitude toward traditional literature reaches a peak in his important article, "Tragedy in Old Chinese Drama," published in English in the inaugural issue of the Shanghai journal *T'ien Hsia Monthly* in 1935. In this first attempt to engage in systematic comparison between Chinese and Western literature, Qian makes little effort to defend the native variety. He begins the piece by claiming flatly that "Whatever value our old dramas may have as stage performances or as poetry, they cannot as dramas hold their own with great Western dramas."[9] Following an idea Wang Guowei first developed in writing about *Honglou Meng* [Dream of the Red Chamber], Qian attributes this to the fact that Chinese drama lacks real tragedy, the highest form of drama. Chinese drama is instead romantic, consisting not of one great passion but of a series of passions strung together. It always contains "poetic justice," but, "of the tragic sense, the sense of pathos touched by the sublime, . . . the knowledge of universal evil as the result of partial good, there is very little trace." Hence the effect on the audience is sadness rather than tragedy: the reader of the plays "goes away from them not with the calm born of spent passions or what Spinoza calls *acquiescentia* with the workings of an immanent destiny, but, on the contrary, haunted by the pang of personal loss, acute, disconsolate, to be hidden away even from oneself " (38).

Echoing his comments on *Odes to the Setting Sun,* Qian further explicates the differences between the Chinese and Western theater by contending that, in the former,

we are not lifted beyond personal sympathy to a higher plane of experience. . . . Instead of a sense of reconciliation and fruition, [Chinese dramas] leave us at the end weakened by vicarious suffering, with a tiny ache in the heart, crying for some solace or support and a scheme of things nearer to the heart's desire. (38–39)

The specific causes of this failure lie in weakness of characterization:

One is unable to rise beyond a merely personal sympathy with the tragic characters because they are not great enough to keep us at a sufficient distance from them. The tragic flaw [*hamartia*] is there, but it is not thrown into sharp relief with any weight of personality or strength of character. (38–39)

Conflict in Chinese drama stems not from the flaw itself or "any decree of fate," but is strictly an *outward* struggle between opposing forces in society, hence the weakness. Noting that Irving Babbitt[10] claimed the supposed lack of "ethical seriousness" in China as the reason for this lack of tragedy, Qian contends that the root cause is rather the strict hierarchy of Confucian values: when one virtue is held to be absolutely higher than another, the lower one is doomed to fail. As a result, the notion of fate available to the Chinese dramatist is in reality no more than simple "poetic justice." Qian points out that A. C. Bradley had carefully distinguished this quality from "Tragic justice":[11]

[The Chinese] conception of Fate is the equivalence of action and award rather than that of cause and effect. It is not the ethically neutral idea that the doer must suffer, but the sentimental belief that virtue is its own reward. [The irony of this fate, then,] is not awful, but petty, malign and "coquettish," as Hardy says of Providence. (44)

In spite of this rather devastating critique, Qian affirms that he makes it without prejudice, that he is essentially "on the side of the ancients," but that the comparison had to be drawn for two reasons. First, careful study of Chinese literature will lead to new *"dogmata critica"* for a universal theory of literature. This, in turn, will eventually produce an understanding of why traditional Chinese critics did not seize upon what Westerners believed to be fundamental critical principles. Second, such open-eyed criticism will enable the Chinese literary world to recognize its own deficiencies. This article, however, goes beyond contributing to Qian's announced goal of literary self-definition. In line with his announced task of probing to the roots of differences in literary values, it also explores some of the social bases underlying them. His assessment of the hierarchical nature of Confucianism is part of this broader analysis; reference to Whitehead's equation of the essentially nonfatalistic nature of tragedy with the Western spirit of science is another.[12]

Qian's erudite "Foreword" to C. D. Le Gros Clark's translation of Su Dongpo's prose-poetry *(fu)* was also published in 1935. The introductory remarks about the intellectual atmosphere of Su's times anticipate the interest in the Song dynasty that culminated in the annotated edition of Song poetry produced by Qian some twenty years later. His interest is, however, decidedly ambivalent. He characterizes intellectuals of the period as "inquisitive rather than speculative," resulting in an "intellectualism" that has "no sweep, no daring, no roominess or margin."[13] But this very intellectualism gives rise both to a greater deliberateness within Song poetry and to the development of practical literary criticism in the form of the burgeoning *shihua* form (which Qian translates here as "causeries on poetry"). This deliberateness causes Qian to regard Song poetry as "sentimental" in Schiller's sense, as distinct from that of the Tang, which Qian calls "naive."[14]

It is perhaps not unreasonable to speculate that Qian's concern for the Song reflects his own position in Chinese history: he is certainly guilty of the overcerebration which he finds in the Song, and the problem of how to create literature anew after the passing of a great age is something that all modern Chinese writers faced, regardless of their conscious disposition toward the tradition. Qian's sympathy for the Song is underscored by his comment that "the most annoying things about . . . [Song poets are] their erudition and allusiveness, which make the enjoyment of them to a large extent the luxury of the initiated even among the Chinese" (xviii). This from a man whose prolific use of allusion dominates his prose style.

Qian departed for England in 1935 and began work on his Oxford degree. Probably because of the time spent in research, he published little during the three years he was in Europe. Of course, given the vagaries of Chinese publishing in the 1930s and the chaos attending upon the outbreak of war in 1937, it is possible that Qian wrote for publication or had published more articles during this period than now survive.[15]

The main effort of Qian's years in Britain was expended on a B.Litt. thesis which was eventually published in three installments in the *Quarterly Bulletin of Chinese Bibliography* in 1940–41. The articles trace rather drily the treatment of things Chinese by British writers before the birth in England of sinology as an academic specialty. While the series does not deal with literary issues in any sustained way, the theme of the problematics of one culture looking at another with any accuracy comes through very strongly: the same China that had been so much admired in pre-1700 England became the object of bemused condescension in the following century. The change had nothing to do with events in China or even with increased contact between the United Kingdom and the Qing empire; it was rather a reflection of fashion and of an increased skepticism toward continental writers laudatory of China. These articles not only give evidence of Qian's concern with cultural relations between China and the West, but also sound a pessimistic note on the incommensurability of cause and effect, something Qian represents with great complexity in his fiction.

Upon his return from Europe, Qian occupied himself with the four major works that will be the subjects of chapters three through six. The only shorter piece of criticism that seems to survive from this period is an introduction to Chinese literature for Western readers published in the *Chinese Year Book* of 1944–45. As this article, abbreviated as it is, is the only comprehensive treatment of all genres of Chinese literature by Qian that is available, it is worth treating at some length. Qian begins the essay by pointing out the length of the tradition and the inevitable staleness which sets in unless it is exposed from time to time to foreign "curiosities." The new literature after the May Fourth movement looks to Western literature out of a healthy impulse for renewal. He is careful to add, however, that "the New Literature, in spite of foreign debts contracted and foreign influences submitted, is at its best as homemade, as racy as the old literature. '*L'influence ne crée rien; elle éveille.*' "[16]

Qian begins the main body of his discussion with poetry, bringing up both the brevity characteristic of the genre and the idea of "poetry as the art of restraining one's emotions" (*shi zhe chi ye*) (119). But whereas in his review of Zhou Zuoren's book, he looked at these notions in their pejorative light, he now takes them positively. Thus, "pure lyricism or *lyricita*, the quintessence and summit of poetic consciousness, appears very early in Chinese literature," and so far from being regarded as a limitation, this phenomenon is seen as indicative of

> The very same precocity [that] can be discerned in other branches of Chinese civilization, which seems to grow on the sunny side of the wall. Chinese pictorial art has reached the stage of pure painting such as was developed by Impressionism and Post-Impressionism in the West long before it perfects the technique of creating realistic illusion. Chinese philosophy boasts of a supple dialectic method while Chinese logic remains elementary. (117)

Similarly, "poetry as restraint" is seen as analogous to classicism. Qian brings up once more the question of "naive" and "sentimental" poetry, holding that most Chinese poetry fits into the former category, as Chinese poets in general are less "sicklied over with metaphysical reflection than their Western confreres. In dealing with such poets of light specific gravity, *glissez et n'appuyez pas* should be the motto of the critic" (120).

The next section deals with the drama. It largely rehearses the arguments made in his *T'ien Hsia Monthly* article and forthrightly sums up by labelling the drama as the crudest of all Chinese literary forms. He proceeds to discuss fiction, the only seriously critical evaluation of that genre that he seems to have published. He begins by making several points. First, that "Chinese novels have as a rule large canvasses and contain dozens of well-delineated characters, not to mention dummies and lay figures. The reason is not far to seek. Most Chinese novels are picaresque. Even the *Red Chamber Dream* is a 'chronicle' and not a 'dramatic novel' " (124). Second, that "the historical element predominates in Chinese fiction. . . . [*Romance of the Three Kingdoms*] *Sanguo Yanyi* is indeed so veracious as to be triumphant proof that historical fiction need not be very unhistorical and fictitious in order to be highly entertaining." Both of these points, as *Fortress Besieged* demonstrates, figure in Qian's own contributions to the new Chinese fiction. He goes on to maintain that authors "rarely ostensibly deal with what is contemporary to them," and that love is similarly rarely of central concern. He contends that the dominant narrative mode is impersonal:

It possesses to an eminent degree the medieval characteristic of anonymity. . . . [I]n the long novels, *Ichroman* or autobiographiction is almost non-existent. In the rare cases of *autobiographie romancée* . . . the author's ego under the conventional disguise of the third person is treated with such a cold detachment and aesthetic distance as to constitute a veritable feat of jumping out of one's own skin. (126)

Again, this statement is highly relevant to Qian's own fiction.

He becomes somewhat more trenchant when he observes that

There is no novel of pure humor in Chinese, but a good deal of social satire, . . . but the Chinese satirists glide off the surface and never probe into the essential rottenness of human nature. They accept the traditional values, social and moral, believe in the innate goodness of man, and poke gentle fun at what they regard as unfortunate backsliding from probity and decorum. They lack that clear-sighted and dry-eyed misanthropy which understands that "the best of men are but men at the best." Just as the Chinese dramatists have no sense of "tragic justice," so the Chinese satirists also lack that terrible *saeva indignatio* which like fire can purify the filth it touches. (125–26)

This assessment echoes both the early Wang Guowei and Qian's own earlier Blakean call for a greater literary dynamism; it perhaps cuts closest to Qian's own attitude toward fiction writing. Combined with his highly negative evaluation of the traditional essay ("It is destined to be the chosen form of the minor writers. Pose, aesthetic trivialism, a lurking fear of the grim realities of life, and an excessive pre-occupation with *bagatelles et bibliots* are the bane of the Chinese essay" [127]), there accrues a good deal of evidence that Qian's reference to the "sunny side of the wall" does not entirely lack irony, that he seeks somewhat more "stress" than he is able to find in traditional Chinese literature. His concluding remarks provide the strongest evidence for this view.

This conclusion begins by repeating the theme that

The New Chinese Literary Movement was only the coming to a head of things. The Chinese literary history of the last thirty years seems a foreshortening of the history of literary movements in Europe of the last two centuries on the biological principle that ontogeny repeats phylogeny. . . . Chinese literature, aroused from its customary slow motion, seems to catch up and match the younger literature of the West. . . .
This acceleration of the pace of Chinese literary history shows one thing. The old literature is not dead, nor is the new literature powerless to be born. True, it is "fecund in abortions." But the best is yet to be, of course. After all, what is thirty years? (127)

He follows with the observation that the great war which had just passed would provide a rich fund of experience to be transformed into literature. This new, dynamic attitude toward literary representation is summed up when Qian contends that the

Chinese would no longer be content to say, " *'Aber wir lassen es andere machen* [But let others do it].' " He concludes the essay with a careful mixture of hope and irony: "A historian of literature is a Leibnizian optimist like Pangloss. He believes that whatever may be the tendency of the post-war literature, whether saying 'yea' to life or 'nay,' Chinese literature will be enriched and its panorama enlivened" (128).

Qian continued to live in Shanghai after the war and wrote much of his work in English, which he published in the quarterly *Philobiblon,* of which he was the editor. Qian has either long reviews or substantive articles in six of the seven numbers of the journal which appeared during its short life. Of these, the most interesting is the essay, "The Return of the Native," where Qian expostulates on a few of the features of the mysticism which remained one of his concerns from the time of his review of "Odes to the Setting Sun." He makes the point that return *(gui)* is used as a metaphor in all Daoist and Chanist mysticism for the mind's process of finding ultimate knowledge in itself. In the course of his exposition, he makes a number of provocative statements that challenge conventional wisdom. Commenting on the elaborateness of Daoist and Buddhist images of death, for instance, he says that their

eloquence is that of a man who stands in secret fear of death, who needs to have the fear lulled by fine words and allows himself to be persuaded death is not death but something else. Confucius' attitude is more courageous: he faced death squarely and called a spade a spade. "If I could discover *Tao* in the morning, let death come to me that very night."[17]

Even more striking, however, are remarks that bear directly on Qian's own writing style. The first page of the article, for instance, consists of a warning against the dangers of using metaphor in rigorous thought: "Metaphor, which is the making of a poet, may prove the undoing of the philosopher" (17). This utterance, while not disqualifying the metaphor that is so much a part of Qian's narrative style, does call ironic attention to its prevalence in his expository prose. Later in the essay Qian brings the reader to a start when he says, apropos of Lessing and Malebranche, that

> I must deny myself the cheap pleasure of generalizing about differences between the Eastern and Western mentality. But to pursue truth for the fun of the pursuit [as do Lessing and Malebranche] is to pursue not truth, but fun; it might be compared to a kitten's sportive chase of its own tail, though such a comparison would do that unpretentious animal some injustice. (21)

Qian's constant resort to cross-cultural comparison and the evident exuberance of his style must give his reader pause to wonder whether or not the author is not having a bit of fun at his own expense here. I think, however, that the more earnest intent of such passages is to have the reader consider what constitutes legitimate "generalizing" and whether the fun in Qian's writing is underscored by something other than mere frivolity. As always with Qian's writing, rumination of the paradoxes he sets is part of the reader's task.

Qian's most important article in Chinese from this period is his "Zhongguo Shi yu Zhongguo Hua" [Chinese Poetry and Chinese Painting], a work that has since been reprinted at least three times. Qian makes a number of points in it about both aesthetic theory and the environment in which art is produced. Before treating these topics, however, he first comments upon the question of tradition itself and its mutability, a subject of vital concern to post–May Fourth Chinese culture. He describes the basic paradox of any tradition:

> Traditions are not willing to change, so they give birth to varieties of formal regulations and habits, taking the contingent and standardizing it. [But] traditions cannot help changing, so many of the formal regulations and habits give birth to varieties of transformations which compromise with and recognize new phenomena. Traditions are living entities rather than dead things.[18]

Thus the more firmly a tradition is established, the more receptive it will be to new things, but the weaker it is, the more it will refuse to admit of the contingent, in spite of its greater need to do so. In the latter case, if a new audience arises which is at too great a variance with the tradition, there will be a "revolution," or cultural crisis.

However,

establishing this new fashion creates an opposing dialectic. On the one hand, there is of course the desire to express an absolutely new spirit, and there are contradictions everywhere with the tradition which is to be overturned. On the other hand, there is the desire to express the fact that one has a historical basis: the past is searched for an [alternative] tradition to be the source of one's work.

Qian, however, compares the latter process to "a bastard seeking his father or a parvenu establishing a pedigree," adding that the search for the "sources of modern literature" set off by Zhou Zuoren in the 1930s was just such a process. Thus he seems to deny in the most sarcastic manner he can muster the legitimacy of using the literature of the past as a basis upon which to build a new literature. A few sentences later, however, he apparently reverses this position by saying that

when a tradition is completely destroyed, the new fashion and the new education contribute to man's habitual forgetfulness. We may, therefore, be able to create a more objective criticism of traditional works of literature. This type of criticism perhaps will grant new knowledge to authors, perhaps will have a great *actualité* for them—are not the so-called "immortal works" those which continue this sense of *actualité*, those which can stand this re-appraisal? (2)

After taking away with one hand the basis for using traditional literature to create the new one, he gives it back with the other. The lesson is, of course, that the difference between illegitimate links and real, organic ones is very fine and that the process must be undertaken with the utmost care.

From these provocative introductory remarks Qian moves to the substance of the essay. He sets out from the commonplace that poetry and painting are regarded as "sister arts" in both

China and the West, but demonstrates that when Chinese and Western aestheticians speak of "poetry in painting" they mean two quite different things: in China this "poetry" refers to a particular lyrical feeling residing in a painting, whereas in Europe it means that the painting contains depictions of events (4). Qian then shows that once modern Western critics became aware of the Chinese idea of lyrical painting, they regarded it as being a product of the same aesthetic sense lying behind both the flexibility and nuance of Southern Chan Buddhism and what they esteemed to be the identical qualities of Chinese poetry. Having established this point, however, Qian once again draws attention to the difference between the standards of judgment of East and West by affirming that traditional Chinese commentators saw the great tradition of Chinese poetry as being based on entirely different grounds:

They would have told us that the great Chinese poets such as Li [Bo (701–761)], Du [Fu (712–770)], Han [Yu], Meng [Jiao (751–814)], Wen [Tingyun (812?–870?)], Li [He (791–817)], Su [Dongpo], Huang [Tingjian (1045–1105)], Bai [Juyi (772–846)] and Lu [You (1125–1210)], for all their differences, gained their power from realism; they were not light and remote, but had color and could create shapes; they did not advocate the ethereal but, rather, weight and thoroughness. (8)

In fact, for all the talk about "sister arts," traditional Chinese theory had different standards for poetry and painting: the solidity of Du Fu was the norm for poetry in a way that the equal solidity said to characterize the painting of Wu Daoxuan (Wu Daozi, d. 792) never was for the latter art. Similarly, the lightness attributed to Wang Wei's (701–761) brush brought him a preeminence in painting theory from which his equally light touch in poetry disqualified him. Qian ingeniously explains this difference in standard in a way that touches upon the fundamentals of general aesthetic theory:

All art has materials which it uses as media of expression. These materials have a given nature which can be used to advantage in expression but which also pose obstructions to limit expression. Artists, therefore, always wish to overcome these limits, to not be tied down by their materials, to force these materials to give shape to a world to which they are not suited. For instance, the medial materials of painting are color and line, which can depict concrete images; [but] great painters just for this reason do not wish to depict images but wish instead to use painting to "show their feelings." The medial materials of poetry are words, which are able to set forth feelings and meanings; [but] just for this reason great poets do not give themselves over completely to "expressing intent," but want poetry to encompass the function of painting and to give their readers images. Poetry and painting both try to jump clear of their natural homes. (14)

The Years after 1957

Soon after the publication of this article began a decade in which Qian largely disappeared from the literary scene. He returned to it rather dramatically in 1957 with the publication in the new journal *Wenxue Yanjiu* [Literary Research] of two excerpts from the book that was to appear the following year as *Song Shi Xuan Zhu* [Annotated Anthology of Song Poetry]. The book contains a representative collection of poems of the major poets of a dynasty that most modern Chinese scholars look to only for the lyrics *(ci)* that conventional literary history had assigned to it as its chief glory.[19] Qian arranges the poems chronologically and at the head of each author's set briefly introduces information pertinent to that author's work. These short notes brilliantly outline the formal influences on each poet as well as how his work relates both to established literary schools and to the work of his contemporaries. As in any such collection, especially one of writers as prolific as those of the Song, selection of individual poems is difficult. The relatively large number of poems on political themes, however, as well as the virtual lack of any discussion of Buddhist influences on the poets, perhaps indicate the influence on Qian of the changed political circumstances of post-1949 China.

Aside from carefully reconstructing literary genealogies, Qian also wrote a general introduction which surveys some of the major issues of Song literary history. Written in the 1950s, when there prevailed in China rather primitive notions of literary evolution and of the relationship of literature to society, Qian's introduction stands as a discussion of these matters possessing textbook clarity. In setting the ground rules, he allows that the Song was beset by enfeebling political difficulties, but also warns against looking to literature for a simplistic reflection of them; literature should not be confused with historical documents. Historical writing demands fidelity to surface reality[20] while

creative literature can dig up the hidden true qualities of things and indirectly relate the unrevealed psychology of people; otherwise it does not fulfill its responsibility as art and it forfeits its position as creative art. Empirical research can only verify what happened, while art can imagine why it should be and suppose why it happened as it did. (4–5)

Qian eventually turns his discussion to the vexing matter of the relationship between Tang and Song poetry. Anticipating Harold Bloom's notion of the "anxiety of influence," Qian notes the difficulties Song poets had in overcoming the sense that the great age of the Tang had exhausted all possibilities for poetry. But he also takes account of the positive side of this imposing heritage: it served as a challenge for later poets to rise to. He sums up the situation with dialectical finesse:

Having Tang poetry as a model was the great good fortune of the Song, but it was also its great ill fortune. Having this model, Song poets could learn their lessons and seek even greater perfection of technique and language. But at the same time, they could also grow lazy because of this model and give free rein to imitation and the inertia of dependence. (13)

Qian cites the Ming critic He Jingming's (1483–1521) condemnation of Song poetry for imitating Tang verse without achieving likeness, something which to Qian is evidence that at least some Song poets overcame the formidable legacy of the earlier dynasty. The differences between the two literatures indicate an originality in the Song far superior to the slavish imitation of Tang forms that Qian regards as characterizing Ming and Qing poetry. He does admit, however, that it is in the Song dynasty that excessive allusion, always a danger in Chinese poetry, became the norm and fostered the sort of academic poetry which modern critics find so objectionable in the work of Ming and Qing authors.

This introduction, then, gives evidence of Qian's ongoing attention to the problem of relating the Chinese tradition to contemporary concerns. He even cites an apposite passage from Mao Zedong's "Yan'an Talks" about the need to innovate while basing oneself on tradition (15). The mercurial Qian of the 1930s has settled into a rather conciliatory role. Events in China since the publication of this 1958 book, however, underscore the importance of such calm attempts to provide access to the richness of the Chinese literary heritage to a society in the convulsions of political and cultural revolution.[21]

From 1958 until 1965 Qian was fairly active. In addition to being in charge of the Tang-Song section of the *History of Chinese Literature* issued by the Literature Section of the Chinese Academy of Sciences in 1962,[22] he published a number of short articles and reviews. One of these, "Tonggan" [Synaesthesia], introduced a number of examples of this phenomenon from both Chinese and Western literature.[23] Qian concludes that the literary use of synaesthesia is not as widespread in China as in the West, in spite of its frequent appearance in Daoist and Buddhist poetry. An essay also published in 1962 entitled "Du 'Laaokong' " [Reading *Laocoon*] represents a much richer comparison of Chinese and Western aesthetic theory; it also continues in the vein of "Chinese Poetry and Chinese Painting" in discussing the specific features of each form. Qian outlines Lessing's distinctions between the two in *Laocoon*—that poetry is uniquely able to express continuity and relations of feeling, while painting's forte lies in its capability to depict one pregnant moment rather than a whole process, a climax or the aftermath of the process.

Qian expands upon this by asserting that the written word is also well suited to portrayal of such pregnant moments, citing the seventeenth-century critic Jin Shengtan's theory of narrative: " 'Writing at its best directs its attention to a particular point and writes no farther, having brought things from far off to this point: the narrative winds its way to the point where something is about to happen and then stops.' "[24] Qian points out that although Jin must distort the nature of traditional Chinese narrative to come to this conclusion—by disingenuously maintaining that all conclusions and climaxes in the great works of narrative and drama were the work of later forgers—the suspenseful endings at the end of each chapter in the episodic novels do avail themselves of the advantages of this technique. The idea can also be most fruitfully applied to Qian's own narrative writing.

The last article Qian published before the Cultural Revolution, "Lin Shu de Fanyi" [The Translations of Lin Shu],[25] discusses issues both of translation and of literary communication, as well as the problem peculiar to Chinese of the gap between language suitable to the purposes of narrative and that restricted by the rules of the so-called "ancient-style" prose *(guwen)*. Beginning with some gnomic remarks on the inevitable distortions of translation, Qian moves on to approve of the liveliness of Lin Shu's style as compared to the original Dickens.[26] Although acknowledging Lin's sin of misrepresentation, Qian credits the continuing readability of the translations to the creative transformation wrought by Lin's reworking the originals in light of traditional canons of Chinese prose. The most interesting part of the article, however, is that which treats of Lin Shu as a stylist of the "ancient-style" school. Qian notes that the term *guwen* has two possible interpretations, one a broad one which refers only to principles of composition, under which rubric no less a personage than the scholar Ruan Yuan (1764–1849) had recognized fictional works such as *Rulin Waishi* [The Scholars]. This definition is no doubt the one Lin Shu himself had in mind when he affirmed that Western fiction contained "ancient-style" prose in its original form (80–81).

The other definition, however, is the strict one of Fang Bao (1668–1749) and his epigones of the Tongcheng school of prose, which not only prohibited all traces of the colloquial language, but most types of literary Chinese as well. This strict standard was bound to hinder severely any narrative style, and Qian finds in Lin Shu's early translations evidence of conflict between the strictures of the Tongcheng style and the requirements of narrative prose for flexibility in representation (86). Qian concludes the article with characteristic iconoclasm: against the conventional wisdom that Lin Shu was an influential apologist for fiction within the most conservative sphere of Chinese letters,[27] he adduces evidence that Lin saw his translations as intellectually justifiable only so far as they led his readers to an appreciation of more orthodox forms of *guwen*. Lin would have been aghast had he seen his work interpreted instead as a bridge leading from a stiff Qing dynasty literary language to the modern vernacular (90).

The points Qian raises in his critical articles over the years between 1932 and 1965 are variously ingenious, but it is possible to discern in them a core concern with the vital topics of the relationship of Chinese literary tradition both to Western theory and, more nebulously, to the possibilities for the continuity of Chinese literature in an age of social and intellectual chaos. His attitudes vary and he often submerges his points in witty pursuit of apparent trivialities, but a commonality of purpose is always there. That purpose is only fully articulated, however, in his longer works, and it is to them that we now turn.

Chapter Three
Tan Yi Lu

Qian Zhongshu's monumental *Tan Yi Lu* consists of a series of short essays and essay cycles on topics in traditional Chinese poetry and poetics. Although he recently dismissed it as "a young man's work" full of intemperate statements that he should no longer wish to stand behind, it remains in the opinion of many scholars his most important piece of writing. Like Erich Auerbach's magisterial *Mimesis, Tan Yi Lu* was produced during the second World War, when libraries were shut or burned and books in general were difficult to obtain. Like *Mimesis,* too, Qian's work was written while its author was in exile from his customary place of work, and many of its quotations are thus rendered from memory, which accounts for a number of minor errors of misquotation.[1] *Tan Yi Lu*'s sheer number of allusions would be staggering testimony to its author's erudition even had he had ready access to the best libraries in the world. Qian's choice of an obscure classical style in which to write it, as well as its rambling *shihua* ("causeries on poetry," to use his own translation of the term) form, leave it a work of more than ordinary difficulty for the twentieth-century common reader, even if that reader has a decent Chinese education. In fact, it contains a certain deliberate challenge to the reading public which is present in all of Qian's work written during the war years.

The work has often been faulted for a lack of explicit overall structure,[2] and at first glance *Tan Yi Lu* would seem to be the pedant's dream: almost four hundred pages of notes in search of a text. While it is true that Qian nowhere sets out a theory or set of themes that he intends to follow, what appears at first to be an almost random collection of writings that jumps from topic to topic reveals with careful reading a constant concern with certain key ideas in traditional literature. The "text" behind *Tan Yi Lu* is in fact nothing less than the main body of classical Chinese poetics. As a result, the work contains 377 pages of closely reasoned and extremely wide-ranging argument that touches on a significant number of the principal issues of traditional poetics. It would be impossible in one chapter to summarize a book of *Tan Yi Lu*'s complex diversity. I shall have, therefore, to focus my analysis on its characteristic modes of discourse, as well as on those essays from the book which presumptively contribute to Qian's general theory of aesthetics. In this respect I hope that the discussion of *Tan Yi Lu* will also shed some light on the principles behind the creative prose that will be the subject of Chapters 4 through 6.

The eventual sense the reader gains of the book's unity has two facets—one more strictly in the realm of critical theory and the other comprising something which can only be called an aesthetic mood. The former is the more obvious and easy to analyze. It consists of a review of traditional literature and the theory behind it, conducted with the intention of pulling the two fields clear of certain ideas which Qian determines to be damaging to literature as he would define the term. His sense of what literature is results from a broad amalgam of Chinese and Western ideas, the key point of which is to establish the independence of literature from historical or ideological utility. Qian's concern with ascertaining what literature is and, more importantly, what good literature is, and how traditional canons of taste help to illuminate this (or obscure it) is what separates *Tan Yi Lu* from what Qian was many years later to call "the futile pedantry and fanciful literal-mindedness of academic literary scholarship."[3] His intention to make the literary heritage comprehensible and useful to his fellows had been evident as early as the first reviews he had published in *Xin Yue,* when, as I discussed in Chapter 2, he aimed to reconcile that tradition with the need for a renewal of contemporary culture.

There seems to exist as well in *Tan Yi Lu,* however, a more lyrical element, something that Qian touches on directly only in his introduction to the work. This introduction, short though it may be, is, like the surprising outburst at the end of his review of *Odes to the Setting Sun,* one of the few places in his writings where Qian lets down his customary ironic guard to vent his feelings outright. Halfway through, after explaining how the book came to be written, he proceeds to explain how he named it:

Men of old capped their works of literary criticism with the beautiful names of their studies so as to record the place of writing and to celebrate the joy of expression. In this way two felicities could be combined. But I have encountered a time of troubles and live in an unhappy age.[4] The nation is broken and my family is scattered; we have nothing to rely on and no place to rest. I have lost my home and must live in a rented room. The hearth of my ancestors and the trees of my old home now seem but fanciful pavilions and imaginary gardens: I think of them but cannot conjure them up. Du Fu's line, "I, a man without roots, will accompany you in uncertainty,"[5] disheartens me every time I think of it. So I simply picked the name of Xu Zhenqing's book[6] and adopted it without alteration. It is not that I did not wish to add anything [to the title] but that there was nothing to add. This is all to show the futility of these changed times. Where is the raven to stop? Orchids have no soil to root in; the cassia does not beckon.[7] A small plot of land, a simple roof over my head: I lack both. Those who understand will know that beyond these words lies an unspoken "Mourning for Jiangnan";[8] it is not that I wish to compare myself to the preening maidens of a great age.[9]

More than explaining the origins of the name, then, Qian is alluding to a purpose of self-expression infused in the text. The quotations he cites are all concerned with laments for troubled times and lack of self-fulfillment, suggesting concerns that go far beyond detached scholarship. This sense of aesthetic purpose is reinforced by the often elaborate imagery that Qian uses in the main body of the text. It is perhaps not too much to suggest that Qian's desire to make literature autonomous and to incorporate within it the capacity for expression of both self and culture, a sense of the literary heritage as well as of the needs of the present, meet in *Tan Yi Lu,* not just with logical proof, but with affective example.

Setting the Literary Context

Qian begins the book proper with a theoretical disquisition on one of his enduring themes: the removal of the province of Chinese literature from its traditional subservience to rigid Confucian historicism. Taking up the theme he first broached in his "Foreword" to C. D. LeGros Clark's *The Prose Poetry of Su Tung-po*,[10] Qian goes about this by first establishing the fact that Tang and Song dynasty poetry each have internal processes of development that are not necessarily linked to the secular history of the societies which produced them:

> I say that when one talks of poetry one should go to the poems themselves. It is proper to mark poetic eras on the basis of form, but it is not necessary to tally these with the vicissitudes of court politics or national events. . . . [So], of course Tang poetry has early, flourishing, middle and late periods, but these do not coincide with the early, flourishing, middle and late periods of history.

Taking the argument further, Qian does allow that differences exist between what have traditionally been classified as Tang and Song poetry, but these are "not only distinctions based on dynasty, but on temperamental differences [of the poets]. There are two types of people in the world and there are thus two types of poetry." He accepts the general distinction that had been made between Tang poetry as more concerned with feeling and Song poetry as more intent upon ideas and structures. Qian is careful, however, to make clear that "the dynastic distinction is only a generality, a convenience of terminology: it is not that 'Tang' poetry is necessarily the product of Tang people or that 'Song' poetry is necessarily the product of Song people" (2). In support of this contention, he cites Du Fu, Han Yu and Meng Jiao as Tang men who originated the mode conventionally associated with the Song, and Pan Dalin (?–after 1193) and Jiang Kui (?1155–?1221) as men of Song who wrote in the "Tang" style.

Qian goes on to equate the two types of Chinese poetry with those referred to in Schiller's distinction between the naive and the sentimental: "All poetry belongs to one of two schools. Ancient poetry is unpolished and natural; modern poetry is intricate and self-conscious. The one emphasizes its virtue, the other, technique. . . . The so-called distinction between ancient and modern has nothing to do with time; it is a matter of style" (3). All poetry after the Song can be sorted in this fashion, but even pre-Tang poetry, "although indistinct as to category and not yet having developed the distinction, can also be sorted in this manner" (4). Qian completes the argument by demonstrating that this difference in temperament can also manifest itself in the same person at different times in his or her life: "Tang" style is characteristic of energetic youth while that of the Song is associated with the more contemplative mood that comes with age. His example is the Ming poet-critic Wang Shizhen (1526–1590).

The above sequence of discussion is clear and straightforward. The same cannot be said, however, for most of the rest of the text. More characteristic by far are oblique lines of argument which touch on a number of topics as they meander along, topic leading to topic almost as if by free association. It is as if Qian's wish to avoid the dogmatism of some traditional criticism leads him to allow the reader to examine every relevant point with a minimum of authorial interference. At times this authorial deference results in what appears to be a lack of any structure at all. In some of the more successful essay-cycles, however, this establishes a creative relationship between text and reader more associated with literature than with literary criticism: the reader must make some effort to construct the argument out of a profusion of building-blocks artfully distributed around him. In this way, *Tan Yi Lu* partakes of a long tradition in Chinese criticism, whose fountainheads include poems about poetry like Lu Ji's (261–303) *Wen Fu* and Sikong Tu's (837–908) *Shi Pin*.

A case in point is the passage which begins with an evaluation of the Qing critic Jiao Xun's (1763–1820) notion that words alone are not sufficient for the full expression of emotion, but must be chanted or put to music in order to succeed at their task. Jiao maintained that

If it could not be chanted it was not poetry. From the Zhou, Qin, Han and Wei [dynasties] on down to Du Fu and Bai Juyi, although styles differed, this precept was not flouted. But with the late Tang, the lyric began to exhaust itself and there was not sufficient feeling to draw upon. Poetry *(shi)* and prose thereupon became confused with one another and the essence of poetry was lost. Sentiment, however, did not end and its expression could not be restrained. As a result, the field was divided and the *ci* ("lyric meter") grew. *Ci* was called "the poetic remnant." Poetry depleted itself in the Song and its essence came to lodge in the *ci*. *Ci* depleted itself in the Yuan and its essence came to lodge in the *qu* ("song-poem"). (32–33)

Qian takes note of the prevalence of this idea, and then goes on to point out the contradictions within it. He holds that, although

shi, ci and *qu* were at first one with music, they proceeded from being one entity into being distinct from one another. Unity in the beginning until eventual separation: all things are like this; how can there be any exceptions? Words and music each have their strong points. The materials and functions of each art have their own directions. In the understanding of them it is difficult to combine the two; if one forces them together, the best of each will not emerge. In fact, it is possible that they will each be harmed. (33)

To illustrate the consequences of this confusion, Qian makes one of the inspired similes for which he is famous. He says that conflating two distinct entities is like mixing black and white paints to create gray and then denying any further need for pure blacks and whites.

After dilating further on the differences between music and poetry, Qian abruptly switches focus to the question of genre depletion, one of the oldest commonplaces in Chinese criticism. This is the idea that each age has a particular form of literature at which it excels. With the full exploration of the possibilities of that form in that age, the genre inevitably gives way to a new one, which is in turn developed to the point beyond which there is nothing more to be done with it. Qian cites a number of the almost innumerable instances of the theory. While this idea is clearly the general case behind Jiao Xun's formulation of *shi, ci* and *qu* (and, for that matter, behind the distinction between Tang and Song poetry), Qian has brought the reader to exposition of the general case only after outlining some of its consequences. During the preliminary discussion of Jiao Xun's point, moreover, he gave no hint as to the eventual direction of his argument. Perhaps, however, it is only through such argument by juxtaposition that Qian can break through the barriers of entrenched conventional wisdom which surround such ideas as that of genre depletion; conventional development, which begins with the major premise and then proceeds to bolster it piece by piece, is not as apt to catch the reader with his prejudices down as is this sort of lateral attack.

After his citation of the arguments of the numerous advocates of the theory of genre depletion, Qian goes on to demolish it:

> Change in literary form is not necessarily to be compared to the metabolic process of living things, in which the old must give way before the new. Parallel prose, for example, was greatly practiced in the Six Dynasties and was eventually replaced with [ordinary] prose. In the Tang ancient-style prose was in vogue again and the masters mostly forsook parallel prose for the ordinary variety. Parallel prose, however, did not thereupon vanish, but continued along in an unbroken stream; although in the Ming it was very little in evidence, it suddenly blossomed forth again during the Qing. In the Qing parallel and ordinary prose coexisted, each achieving its own glory. The Yanghu and Yangzhou prose schools even advanced a theory of combining the two.[11] So where is the evidence that the rise of one implies the fall of the other?
>
> Furthermore, to use the example of the "eight-legged" essay, its syntax is based on parallel prose, while its form of composition was born of the drama. How can one then say that the eight-legged essay arose while parallel prose and the drama both died out? And how do the transformations of poetry and the *ci* lyric differ from this? (35)

Qian closes this part of his argument with a flurry of images, again something more characteristic of an aesthetic than a critical mode of discourse. He suggests first that those who preach the depletion theory run the risk of being dismissed themselves as being unable to create new poetry. He compares them to defeated generals who blame the fates for their catastrophes and to toppled rulers who use the heavenly mandate as the excuse for their destruction. Qian adds that for all such resigned people, there is a certain number who are willing to challenge the fates or to set up new dynasties. The Tang was a time when people of the latter type lived, but since then there have been all too many who have followed the errors of Jiao Xun and those like him.

Returning to Jiao Xun's notion that poetry was lost because "poetry and prose . . . became confused with one another," Qian changes tack again in order to discredit this idea. He begins by asserting that words and things theretofore not regarded as being fit to include in poetry serve to revitalize that genre once it adopts these new forms of diction. He supports his point by quotations from Western critics and mentions that even Chinese critics singled out Han Yu's use of prosaic language as one of the main virtues of his poetry. Qian caps his argument by showing how Du Fu, the poet so admired by Jiao Xun, when confronted with a poetic rhetoric exhausted by Six Dynasties euphuism, incorporated many prose elements into his poetry. At this point Qian strikes a cadence by sarcastically remarking that for Qing empiricists such as Jiao Xun to attempt to discuss aesthetics is like "a dreamer talking in his sleep" (37).

Qian does not, however, deny the concentration in one dynasty of brilliant works of a particular genre. Thus Wang Guowei's formula of Han *fu*, Tang *shi*, Song *ci* and Yuan *qu*, which holds that

> any one form reaches its height under one dynasty, is all right. But if his intention is the same as that of Jiao Xun, and he is saying that any one form is restricted to one age and that the number of authors engaged in that form is proof of the quality of what they produce, then this is the viewpoint of the shopper seeking to get the most weight for his money. (37)

At this point, Qian goes behind the traditional argument to hold that the force of the case for genre depletion is vitiated by the fact that an identical fund of poetical feeling lies beneath all poetic forms. He thus distinguishes between "poetic form and poetic feeling," maintaining that since *shi*, *ci* and *qu* are all lyrical forms anyway, their simultaneous existence is not contradictory.

In spite of Qian's seemingly objective presentation, the careful reader is still left with a sense that the author has begged the question of why certain forms do predominate in certain times, a fact that he has grudgingly admitted to be true. If *shi, ci* and *qu* are all but the external manifestation of a consistent lyrical sensibility which is even at times shared with prose, why should authorial preference change over time? Changing habits and ways of life, the development of new forms, not to mention overuse of certain sets of images or themes associated with trite convention, may, from the standpoint of the aspiring poet, in fact render forms "obsolete." Qian does not make clear just how he envisages the differences between various lyrical forms. If all the genres at any given time possess the same capacity for lyrical expression, in what sense do they differ? Is it simply a question of random differences of form? It is true that Qian is intent more on clearing away mechanistic misconceptions about the nature of Chinese poetry, but his solutions bring up certain other problems in turn. His discussion of these issues in the introduction to his anthology of Song poetry is more forthright.

Qian's discussion of genre depletion contains many of the features characteristic of *Tan Yi Lu*'s discourse. First, he marshals extensive evidence in a highly inductive style: the reader is presented with an almost bewildering array of documentation for each point. Second, the arguments have a minimum of connective tissue; one stops and another starts without warning, and little time is wasted explaining why B should follow A. Third, Qian's main points often couch themselves without warning in the middle of a passage rather than at its head or conclusion. Fourth, lyrical passages and paradox are rife. Finally, Qian limits himself to certain points and resists any temptation to make explicitly far-ranging theoretical statements. The combination of these modes of argument is highly effective: it disarms the reader by giving the impression of absolute adherence to fact, such that Qian's conclusions appear to be beyond question. The universality he conjures up out of his combined appeal to Chinese and Western sources makes it difficult to locate Qian's own prejudices. There is nonetheless a penalty exacted for this subtlety: the density and fineness of the argumentation are such as to lie beyond the understanding of most potential readers. And it is presumably such readers who most need the correctives that the book has to offer.

Tan Yi Lu's virtuosity is illustrated by a short passage that comes up in the genre depletion section. Mentioning the subject of the "eight-legged" essay in the course of his discussion of parallel prose, Qian thereupon appends a brief and lucid account of this form, which was used for the old civil-service examinations and was the bane of most modern Chinese literary scholars.[12] Qian boldly attempts to reverse the verdict on this much maligned genre. Beginning by tracing through earlier scholarship the origins of the eight-legged essay in parallel prose and the extension of parallel prose that was the dramatic lyric, he goes on to note that

> the old name for the eight-legged essay was "speaking for" *(dai yan)*, most likely because it sought to mimic the speech of the ancients. It put [the author] in the place [of the person for whom the author was speaking] and developed an essay [on that basis]. It employed the way of the theater to draw forth the spirit of the sages. . . . I should say that if one wishes to gain a glimpse of the feelings and actions of Confucius and Mencius, one must go to the best of Ming and Qing eight-legged essays to find them. The form brings them to life. The commentaries and sub-commentaries of the Han and Song on the Four Books are simply not worthy of discussion [in this regard. But the eight-legged essay's] brilliance of apprehension and subtlety of imagination are of a piece with drama. (42–43)[13]

Moving here beyond the question of subservience to Confucian values (which probably lay behind much of the modern hostility to the form), Qian unearths materials for a tradition of mimesis and narrative continuity out of one of the most unlikely parts of the Chinese literary heritage.

Qian's opinion that some modern attitudes toward literature are as damaging to it as traditional prejudice becomes evident in another appendix to the discussion of genre depletion. In outlining one of his contemporary's mistakes, Qian shows how modern errors of judgment are often extensions of traditional attitudes, a fact that is itself backhanded tribute to the strength of premodern Chinese literary values. Qian begins the appended note by tracing out the social Darwinism present in certain Western theories of genre transformation. He then shifts his ground to quote a modern Chinese scholar to the effect that in ancient times there was no such thing as what we would now call poetry: the scholar is attempting to prove etymologically that *shi* was simply the recording of history (44). Qian sees this claim as arising out of the same Qing dynasty mentality that produced Jiao Xun. After demonstrating how etymological "proofs" have often been in error and that a strictly logical argument cannot discuss the properties of something if one first posits its nonexistence, Qian moves on to the substantive issue—the relationship between literature and history—an important one to traditional criticism that became even more important in twentieth-century thinking dominated by social concerns.

Qian starts this portion of his exposition by pointing out that in ancient times literature and history were not differentiated. From this rather commonplace assertion he goes on suddenly to question the veracity of the Chinese historiographical tradition. His reasoning, if a bit fluid, is based on a wide variety of evidence:

The historical sense of our ancestors was still shallow. They did not know to be skeptical nor to pass down only reliable information, nor could they clarify what was true and separate it from illusion. What are called the "Veritable Records" *(shi lu)* are full of imagined facts. "It must have been so" and "although not certain, it is likely to be true,"[14] retelling the past in such a way as to make it conform to present purposes, talking about another as a fable for oneself—[all of these prove] that "history" is nothing but straight *poiesis*. Thus Confucius said that "when words [*wen*] exceed substance, the result is history," and Mencius said that "believing everything in the [*Classic of*] *History* is worse than having no *History* at all."[15] . . . Looked at from this viewpoint, the ancients possessed poetic minds but lacked historical virtue. Better than saying "ancient poetry is history" would be to say that "ancient history is poetry." (46–47)[16]

As one of his references to justification of factual distortion is from the Song dynasty, Qian clearly means to demonstrate that the ambiguity between historical and literary texts extends throughout Chinese history. He attributes this ambiguity to a universal "will to art" (*Kunstwollen* in the original) (47). Aside from being a remarkable example of the historiographical skepticism that so marked Chinese intellectual life in the period after the May Fourth movement, this paragraph, by turning the traditional relationship of history and literature on its head, expands the scope of literary inquiry almost to infinity. But Qian chooses not to dwell on the matter; his distaste for easy speculation causes him to leave it to the reader himself to draw any more general conclusions. It is enough for him to have piqued the imagination.

The sections just discussed in large part serve as introduction to the more specific issues that predominate in the rest of *Tan Yi Lu*. It is typical of the book's elliptical method that these theoretical segments do not appear consecutively—a long subcommentary on the standard commentary to the Song poet Huang Tingjian's poetry appears in the middle. Neither is there any indication of the thematic importance of these sections. The reader becomes aware of these passages' importance only as the themes introduced therein begin to resonate with the more specific analyses of individual authors and their works that follow.

On Li He

Of these detailed essays, some of the most interesting center on the Tang poet Li He. The passages on Li are almost as amorphous as the rest of *Tan Yi Lu*. One's first impression is that the only thread holding together the twenty pages on Li is simply that each page contains some discussion of Li's poetry or a theoretical issue raised by the poetry. As elsewhere, Qian does not explicitly outline his intentions nor set forth any theoretical framework. He fails to provide any background on Li's life and times—that staple of traditional Chinese literary scholarship— or to give us a single integrated analysis of an individual poem— a more serious offense to the Western reader raised in the ambience of the New Criticism. Qian's treatment demands a level of knowledge of Li in particular and of the tradition of Chinese poetics in general daunting to anyone who does not have at least a thorough knowledge of the Li He corpus.

What Qian does do in his writing about Li He is to give a clear picture of the critical context that surrounds the late Tang poet. For an explanation of why Qian does this, we must turn to the first pages of his 1947 essay "Chinese Poetry and Chinese Painting":

We study the history of criticism for the sake of our own criticism. To comprehend and to evaluate an author we should at times know others' opinions of him. An artist always creates within a certain fashion *(fengqi);* this fashion influences his selection of material, the height of his standards, as well as giving him opportunity and limiting his scope. Even those who are opposed to this fashion receive its negative impetus, because they must open new paths to avoid the fashion they so despise. So fashion is the latent force in creativity; it also forms the background to the work, but it can never be seen in the work itself. All we can do is read the criticism of the author's work by his contemporaries to see what sort of fault they find with it, how they praise it, and what sort of demands and standards they have. Only in this way can we understand just what the surrounding environment is, as we can tell the configuration of the wind from the contours of waves of blowing sand.[17]

Qian's wish to set the record of the past straight, the better to set standards for modern literature, is very clear here.

Qian commences his essays on Li He by mentioning the traditional wariness of Li's supposed "demonic talent" *(guicai).* He shows how the Qing critic Yao Wenxie (fl.ca. 1650) represents the dominant faction of literary opinion in attempting to explain away this ostensible defect by attributing to Li veiled critiques of contemporary politics in what appear on the surface to be bizarre images. Qian objects to this sort of criticism; he cites it as yet another example of the excesses of scholars of literature who lack literary sensibility. He does note, however, that this type of allegorical interpretation of literary texts has a long tradition in China, extending as far back as Confucius's supposed ordering of the *Spring and Autumn Annals* and the *Classic of Poetry.*[18]

Qian begins his refutation of the allegorical interpretation of Li He by pointing out the logical contradiction between the poet's ostensible intention of making his political critique known and the high obscurity of the images themselves: what point satire if no one could understand it? (54). He underscores this argument by remarking how Li He's contemporaries Yuan Zhen (779–831) and Bai Juyi were not afraid to be quite open in their ridiculing of political affairs. Qian also quotes (or rather, misquotes) an ambiguous line from Du Mu's (803–852) preface to Li He's poetry, to the effect that Li did not share Qu Yuan's (?343–278 B.C.) ability to stir social concern.[19] Not that Qian totally denies a certain social consciousness to Li's poetry; he in fact caps his argument with the observation that in those poems where Li does indulge in social criticism, he is—in the tradition of Du Fu— quite open about it (56).

While still dealing with the question of allegorical interpretations, Qian makes a direct comment on Li He's poetry. As one of his reasons for denying allegory, Qian maintains that Li's concern with rhetorical style *(xiuci)* overwhelms his attempts to impart a unified meaning to his poems. Qian cites traditional authority to this effect and then likens Li to a "nearsighted person. From close up he can minutely discern the finest particle, but from afar he cannot make out a cart-load of kindling" (55). This perception—one which is, needless to say, not popular among modern students of Li He[20]—comprises Qian's essential view of Li's poetry. It serves as the underlying theme of the rest of the discussion on Li and as a limit which Qian implicitly places on the poet's literary achievement. It is typical of *Tan Yi Lu*'s style that this key insight should be, as it were, bootlegged into the course of an argument that is at the same time rather random and not overtly concerned with the aesthetic evaluation of the poems themselves.

With this major qualification entered, Qian turns to examine Li He's imagery—the fruits of Li's myopic scrutiny. Once again Qian begins indirectly with a remark about how the nineteenth-century French critic Theophile Gautier, in his critical work *L'Art,* had called poetry *"le bloc résistant."* Taking up this notion of hardness, Qian points out how various Western critics have noticed the use of metals, stone and other hard objects as metaphors in the poetry of Baudelaire, Hebbel, and Poe. Qian regards Li He as the Chinese representative of this category and proceeds to give a full page of examples, commenting at the end of the list that the images are, as a whole, "strange and ragged; all these examples transform things light into things congealed and heavy. They sharpen that which ordinarily flows freely" (58). Qian holds that these hard, cold and dead images represent Li's principal poetic motifs and that, in addition to being hard and dead, Li's imagery is also fraught with tension. Qian asks rhetorically how these two contradictory features can coexist and answers that this is precisely what constitutes Li He's singularity:

The quality of each element is congealed and hard, but the movement of the whole is rapid and flexible. So, if looked at in pieces, the rhetoric is heavy, but if read out all at once, it seems to move. It is not the autumn flood on the Yangzi of Han Yu's poetry, the same for a thousand *li,* nor is it the ten thousand springs of Su Dongpo which gush up everywhere. It is, rather, like the sudden collapse of a mountain of ice or the rapid movement of the Gobi desert—it is a force embracing shards and small stones in forward motion. Although it is a solid mass, it is mobile. (60)

Qian moves from this striking description of effect to explain one of the technical features of its composition. He says that it is a peculiarity of Li's style to have images and the objects which they are replacing sharing only a limited number of characteristics; original and substitute are not of the same class. Abstracting from this limited similarity, Li then attributes features of the first thing to the second that are outside the scope of what they have in common. For instance, Li's "A Ballad of Heaven" contains the line: "Clouds flowing through the Silver Stream mimic the sound of water."[21] Qian remarks of this that "Clouds can be compared to water in that they both flow, otherwise they have nothing in common. But when Li He writes about them, clouds both flow like water and sound like water."[22] Another example is from "The Prince of Qin Drinks Wine": "Xi He [the charioteer of the sun] whips the sun with a glass-like sound."[23] The sun and glass are both bright, but Li extends to the former the noise-making properties of the latter. While this point would seem to lead directly to theoretical disquisition on the nature of Chinese poetic imagery in general, Qian is only concerned with establishing that there is logic to Li He's figures, which traditional critics had chided as "strange and unreasonable." Anything beyond this is left to the reader's speculation.

While Qian's section on Li He's imagery develops in logical sequence as I have set it out here, the same cannot be said about the shape of the discussion in *Tan Yi Lu*. The statement concerning the hardness of Li's images and the passage about a hard mass on the move are separated by a number of apparent digressions on such topics as the uniqueness of Li He's eeriness, a critique of some comments by the early twentieth-century writer Su Manshu and Li's sense—apparently shared with the Greeks—of the futility of offering libations to the dead (59). One is tempted to argue that Qian's concern for the specific, his exhaustive treatment of every issue just at the point that it surfaces—no matter how minor—exemplifies that very myopia he finds in Li He.[24] The emergence of a comprehensive line of analysis after some investment of the reader's time, however, gainsays such an interpretation. It bespeaks, rather, a commitment to the aesthetic contours of traditional *shihua* and *suibi* ("random jottings") style, in which a deliberate looseness of manner encodes an informality intended at once to ingratiate itself with the reader and to avoid the lugubrious authority of formal prose. Qian's concern with the differences between the informal and the formal style—and the advantages of the informal—can be traced back to his 1932 review of Zhou Zuoren's book. This calculated informality is, as we shall see, certainly a predominant feature of his creative work; it is a taste he shares with most writers of the 1930s, who were seeking alternatives to what they regarded as the pernicious tradition of *wen yi zai dao*.[25]

Qian does include a theoretical component in his essays on Li He, although—as with most of his excursions into theory—he places it in a note appended to the main text. The "note," however, runs over six pages and attempts to delineate the relationship between the poet and the objects of his lyrical attention. Qian heads the discussion with his observation that many of Li's lines impute human feelings to non-human objects. The numerous examples include such verses as "Lotuses weep dew as orchids smile" from "Li Ping at the Harp," and "Dark orchid's dew / Like crying eyes" from "Su Xiaoxiao's Tomb."[26] Qian traces the use of this trope in other poets and notes how Li overuses it and thereby vitiates its potential subtlety. His general comment on the abuse of the technique is that

although feeling *(qing)* and scene *(jing)* are both present, there still exists a division between the internal and the external. The lines only accommodate the scenes to [the poet's] feelings and do not see the feelings inhering in the scene. So one may say that [the poet's] mind contains the natural scene, but does not know that the natural scene also contains a mind, which still awaits its true reflection in the poetic mind. (63)

Qian thus makes the distinction between investing objects with the subjective feelings of the author and a mutual interpenetration of the two subjects, in which the mind receives—rather than imposes—the essence of the thing.

In tracing the origins of this fusion between sense and object, Qian cites the "Yong ye" passage from the *Confucian Analects* as one of its earliest sources: "The man of knowledge is active, so he loves water; the man of benevolence is quiescent, so he loves mountains."[27] It is characteristic of Qian's eclectic and nonconforming nature to turn to the *Analects*—a book most literary men of his generation regarded as anathema to an "autonomous literature"—as the *locus classicus* of a key notion in Chinese aesthetics.[28] He sums up the import of the *Analects* passage epigrammatically:

The benevolent and the knowledgeable see benevolence and knowledge in the quiescence of mountains and in the activity of water. Each has its own accord, hence, its pleasure. But the quiescence of mountains is not benevolence itself, nor is the activity of water knowledge. They are separate from one another, and this is why [the benevolent and the knowledgeable] are able to apprehend [these qualities] and to take pleasure in them. (63)

Thus while only mutual penetration of feeling allows feeling to take root, it is only awareness of the ultimate separation between the feeling and the object that allows the innate qualities of the object to be perceived.

It turns out, then, that what Qian finds at the root of his objection to Li's images is that they do not reflect a respect for the integrity of the objects of his attention. Qian sees Li investing things with a consciousness strictly his own, bringing to bear an overwhelming subjectivity that causes Li's "mind to grasp on [to only one aspect of the thing] and not to perceive its myriad manifestations" (67). Qian notes that the consequent distortion of the natures of objects is akin to Ruskin's "pathetic fallacy."

Qian goes on to demonstrate some of the effects these poetical devices have on Li's poetry. Having cited example after example of Li's exotic imagery, Qian observes that such devices, had they been used sparingly, would have retained a certain "cold beauty," but their almost obsessive frequency instead proves to be tiresome. Qian sees in this a determination on Li's part to avoid above all common and prosaic elements in his verse. Echoing his earlier comments about Du Fu's incorporation of prose diction into his poetry, Qian judges that Li's failure to recognize that "everything in the world is [potential] poetry" lies at the heart of what he regards as the poet's ultimate shallowness. Qian takes his final remark about the poetry from one of Li's poems. He cites the last two lines of "Delights of the Jasper Pool"—"And Lead-flower water to wash your very bones: / Here I will sit with you while you grow immortal"[29]—to summarize Li's earnest attempts to transcend the commonplace.

It is only after completing this examination of Li's poetical rhetoric that Qian moves on to analyze Li's themes. He finds the dominant one to be a sense of the dissonance between human fate and the unconcern of nature. Qian mentions that other poets also wrote on this, but that Li He is unique in his desire to halt the whole course of cosmic flux. Qian concisely illustrates Li's singularity by quoting two poems on this theme, one by Li He and the other by his illustrious Tang forerunner, Li Bo. Both are entitled "Ballad of the Rising Sun"; Li Bo's reads as follows:

> The sun rises from the eastern valley
> As if from the bottom of the world.
> Once through the sky it re-enters the sea,
> Where is this residence of the six dragons?
> From of old it has never ceased to be thus.
> Man is not of primeval stuff, how can he long keep pace?
> But grasses do not thank the spring winds for their glory,
> Nor do trees blame the autumn for their fall.
> Who wields the whip to stir on the seasons?
> The myriad things flourish and cease naturally.
> Xi He, Xi He—
> How is it you sink in the wild waves?
> Of what virtue Lu Yang
> To stop the skies with flourish of spear?
> To oppose the way, to go against heaven,
> Your deception is great indeed.
> I shall grab off a great part
> And grandly merge myself with nature.[30]

Li He's more difficult version is:

> White sunlight rises on the Kunlun mountain,
> Sends forth rays like unravelling silk thread.
> It vainly shines on my sunflower heart,
> Not illuminating wanderer's grief.
> The winding Yellow River: at its bend
> Comes the sun wheeling down from mid-sky.
> I have heard of the valley the sun comes from,
> But not seen the western tree in which it sets.
> The heat fuses rocks: what can be done?
> It melts mankind: what is the reason?
> Once Yi did bend his bow and aim his shafts.
> He did not fail to hit the sun-crow's foot
> And leave it still for many lengths of time.
> Why should dawn's rays in evening grow obscure?[31]

Both of these poems are inspired by the "Rising and Setting of the Sun" song of the *Sacrificial Songs of the Han*,[32] and are, like the original, laments on the failure of humans to master nature and their own fates. The similarities, however, end there. Li Bo acknowledges man's inability to come to grips with eternity, but quickly accepts the inevitability of this. He even calls Lord Lu Yang's temporary reversal of the sun's course an action contrary to what should be. He closes his poem on a ringing *carpe diem* note which contrasts sharply both with the poem's beginning and with the Han dynasty source poem.

Li He's ballad contains a much more problematic treatment of the sun and the passage of time it represents. The distance between human and natural process is magnified both by the standard lament about the futility of loyalty and by the uncertainty about how the sun really works in lines 5–8; the sense of the oppressiveness of time is expressed through the image of the sun (or suns) literally melting the earth and its inhabitants away. Li He's final wish to halt natural process altogether runs directly counter to the import of Li Bo's work. As Qian says: "In speaking from the standpoint of a fate which does not reach to the waxing and waning of human affairs, Li Bo approximates Li He. But Li Bo's wish to acclimate himself to this process is wholly at odds with Li He's sense of the passage of time and his wish to halt its rapid passage" (70). Qian closes his comments on Li He with a laconic note on how sadly appropriate it is that these lines of regret for the passing of time should come from the shortlived Li He.

This final evaluation of Li He's work follows the established *Tan Yi Lu* pattern. Qian quotes lines without providing much commentary: the reader is expected to be able to draw his own conclusions from the raw material presented. The few comments Qian does make are in large part lyrical lines from other writers in the same mode as the work that Qian is inspecting. He sums up Li He's attitude toward fate, for instance, by quoting the final two lines from Li Shangyin's quatrain "Sunset Tower": "I wish to ask the lonely wild goose whither it is flying, / Not knowing that my own destiny is just as vague as his."[33] Qian adds to this that Li's life and the poetry he produced "peculiarly cause one's tears to be shed and one's heart to fall," "shedding tears and causing the heart to fall" being phrases from Jiang Yan's (444–505) "Resentment *Fu*" *(Hen Fu)*.³⁴

More striking than anything else, however, is how Qian's essays on Li He are conducted in the terms of traditional poetics. This is not simply a matter of the *shihua* form and the classical language used, but of having the discussion center on the judgments of earlier Chinese critics and of matching Li He's themes and diction with those of his contemporaries. In this, Qian shows both where Li fits into the literary heritage and where he breaks with it. Citing the traditional commentaries has the added advantage of allowing the reader to judge the quality of the commentaries themselves and to become aware thereby of the "fashions" of premodern poetics. The combination of using an individual author's work to illustrate features of the traditional literary environment while at the same time showing how that environment shapes the author is what makes *Tan Yi Lu* a uniquely valuable book. Qian avoids the dual pitfalls of either iconoclastically abstracting an author's work from the tradition and misreading it in light of modern aesthetic theory—something to which Li He's verse is particularly susceptible—or accepting without further examination old critical canons, many of which distort the range of response to literature. Qian's constant comparisons with Western poetics provide a mirror to test the universality of the ideas he examines.

On the Evaluation of Han Yu

This context-building feature of *Tan Yi Lu* is better illustrated by the section on the Tang writer Han Yu which follows the essays on Li He. Beginning by mentioning how most writers from the Northern Song dynasty on regarded Han Yu very highly, Qian goes on to list the views of a number of dissenters from this opinion. After citing a series of statements that criticize some of Han Yu's inconsistencies, Qian enters his own evaluation:

These are all carping, killjoy sorts of utterances. Han Yu's appeal lies precisely in the fact that, although he regarded himself as a student of the *Dao*, both his words and actions were intemperate and his writings lacked any basis [in his behavior]. But this makes him very human. In *juan* 684 of the *Complete Tang Prose*, the "Two Letters of Zhang Ji to Han Yu" forcefully castigate Han Yu's argumentativeness, his desire for erudition and personal advancement and his love of toying with people. Han Yu's replies are all in his collected works, and they are remarkable for their sense of "you go your way and I'll hold to mine." There persists in them an air of magnanimity and frankness which prevents him from disguising the eccentricity that exists in spite of his wish for rectitude. There is a definite difference in quality between him and a punctilious and constricted pedant. (75–76)

Following this, instead of going on to discuss various features of Han Yu's work—as he had done with Li He—Qian presents a selection of comments on Han Yu by post-Tang scholars which informs the reader much more about the commentators and their various concerns than about Han Yu himself.

In the essays that follow, Qian does not shrink from indulging himself in the minutiae of academic discourse. In sorting out the nature of Han Yu's relationship to Buddhism, for instance, Qian dilates at considerable length on Song dynasty opinion concerning the authenticity of Han's letters to the monk Da Dian.[35] Citing various opinions, Qian holds to the view that Han Yu's intercourse with Da Dian resulted from the loneliness of his southern exile rather than from any hidden admiration of the monk's doctrines, as Han Yu's detractors allege. Qian's marshaling of the evidence on this question makes it clear that post-Tang opinion on it was more a matter of the investigator's predisposition toward Han Yu than any rigorous adherence to fact.

Following the discussion of the Da Dian question, Qian begins an extended disquisition on the use of particle words *(xuzi)* in poetry. Echoing one more time his concern with the interplay between poetry and prose, he shows in strictly formal terms the debt of late Tang and post-Tang verse to usages that had earlier been considered the exclusive province of prose. Qian finds particles being used in poetry as early as in the work of Tao Qian (365–427)—something which accounts for his unique style—and traces the increasing use of the practice into the Tang. Han

Yu's contribution was his ability "to gather the best of the syntactical features of the earlier writers" (86) and create a style of great force through the use of particles. Although Han Yu occupies a pivotal place in this exposition, Qian spends almost no time illustrating his point with any lines from Han Yu's poetry, moving on instead to show Han's influence on later poets.

The form of Qian's argument here strikes the reader as being most peculiar. Rather than describing in any general or theoretical way Han Yu's leadership of the archaist *(fugu)* movement, which has been the approach of most critics,[36] Qian limits himself strictly to isolating the formal features that comprise Han Yu's style. Even in this, almost all his examples are from poets who either preceded or succeeded Han Yu. Also curious is the starkly empirical approach that Qian takes; pages 84–85 and 89–90 consist exclusively of examples of lines containing particles. When the discourse shifts to Han Yu, however, Qian dispenses with examples and presents summary judgment. This is no doubt due in large part to Qian's wish to avoid belaboring the obvious: the prosy nature of Han Yu's poetry is a cliché that needs no further airing. What really interests Qian is the historical development of the style, or, in other words, how this well-known feature of Han Yu's work fits into the Chinese poetical tradition.

After a lengthy and rather remote exploration of the effects of particles on later poetry, Qian returns to Song dynasty evaluations of Han Yu, the point at which he began. Coming after the long assessment of Han's influence, however, this section has a more judicious tone to it. Qian notes that such diverse personages as Wang Anshi (1021–1086), Cheng Yi (1033–1107), Zhu Xi (1130–1200), and Lu Jiuyuan (1139–1193) all criticize Han Yu for valuing pure learning over self-cultivation. Qian is quick to add that Cheng, Zhu and Lu all ultimately regard Han positively and accept his self-assessment as the lone transmitter of the Confucian *Dao*. And there is almost universal approbation of Han Yu's prose style. Along with some final remarks on the strict mutual criticism of various Song Neo-Confucianists, this final section of Han Yu shows how the picture of him as a priggish, if quixotic, sort of Chinese Malvolio is more the product of his later interpreters than of measured reaction to his actual behavior.

The net effect of the essays on Han Yu, then, is to demonstrate the extent to which conventional wisdom about Chinese literary figures is the product of factional and ideological considerations at some remove from the texts that the later scholars are purporting to comment on. In the case of history's treatment of Han Yu, Qian shows how the "mutual detestation and over-severity" (100) of Song Neo-Confucianists caused Han's detractors to be particularly sharp in their condemnation. To defend Han in this strict environment, his defenders—whose views were eventually to prevail—were obliged to try to portray him as a paragon of a more rigid code of behavior than was dreamt of in Tang times. Qian thus skillfully demonstrates the ability of purposeful historiography to create biased views of the past. The intricacy and wide range of the exhumation testify both to the complexity of this process of distortion and to its continuing hold over the scholarly imagination.

Criticism on Criticism

In treating Li He, Qian focused more on the individual poet and in expatiating on Han Yu, *Tan Yi Lu* was more concerned with context and the evolution of technique. Another sort of essay cycle in the book takes traditional works of literary criticism themselves as subject. The best and longest example of this latter sort of discussion is Qian's exposition of the Qing critic Yuan Mei's (1716–1798) *Suiyuan Shihua,* which takes up almost a quarter of *Tan Yi Lu.* The section begins, with characteristic indirection, with a rather snide denunciation of Arthur Waley's fondness for the Tang poet Bai Juyi. After a number of desultory remarks that effect a transition to Yuan Mei, Qian delivers a preliminary statement of how he intends to treat *Suiyuan Shihua:*

The main points of Suiyuan's discussion of poetry are known by everyone, so I need not go into them here in detail. In the last hundred-odd years [since Yuan's death] there has been no shortage of castigation of Yuan. Most of this has been of Yuan's "insufficient learning" and of his lack of calm judgment. I, without sufficient reflection, shall base myself on the *shihua* itself and collate miscellaneous matters that previous critics have not gone into. The book is well known and has been on scholars' minds for some time. Of all the *shihua*, none can compare with it. So in my picking out its faults and bringing out its points shared with other works, those who know of what I speak may perhaps find something of value. (233)

In addition to making explicit his determination not to belabor the obvious, Qian implies here a wish to avoid being held the captive of conventional judgments of Yuan Mei. The reader is, however, allowed a certain skepticism in regard to Qian's claim to deal only with "miscellaneous matters." As we have already seen, Qian's apparent randomness of approach in *Tan Yi Lu* masks a series of more earnest concerns.

After these opening remarks Qian plunges into an analysis of Yuan's work. If the sections in *Tan Yi Lu* on Li He and Han Yu tend to ramble, this is even more the case with the essays on *Suiyuan Shihua*. This is appropriate enough, since Yuan's work is a diffuse series of comments on various authors and ideas, and any discussion of it cannot help sharing in part its lack of a fixed center of discussion. Like other *shihua*, *Suiyuan Shihua* consists of a variety of discrete statements, some of which contradict others. Modern scholars have attacked Yuan Mei for this lack of overall consistency, and Qian both admits the truth of the accusations and provides further examples. Qian explains that the inconsistencies probably result from Yuan's "addressing himself to the occasion at hand each time he wished to affirm something; out of a sense of his own heroism, he overcorrects misconceptions" (259). It is noteworthy that Qian's longest section by far should be given to a work of the same form as *Tan Yi Lu*. As mentioned already, accusations of randomness and lack of organization have also been applied to Qian's work. The combination of Qian's use of the *shihua* form and his extensive commentary of *Suiyuan Shihua* indicate his desire to demonstrate the continuing value and possibilities of the traditional form.

For all the surface haphazardness of Qian's treatment of Yuan, however, there is (at least in the first part of the discussion) a constellation of themes upon which Qian focuses. This centers on the relationship of poetic form to theme and includes the related questions of the relationship of Chan Buddhist ideas to poetry and the nature of "poetic sensibility" *(xingling)* and its links to craft. In the course of pointing out some of the inconsistencies in Yuan's pronouncements on these matters, Qian sets forth a number of Chinese and Western opinions on them, mediating between the extremes in attempting to present a balanced view. The discussion is in large part amplification of an earlier passage from *Tan Yi Lu* in which Qian had demonstrated that the "spiritual resonance" *(shenyun)* of the Qing critic Wang Shizhen (1634–1711) dates back to similar ideas of the Tang theorist Sikong Tu and of Yan Yu (fl. ca. 1200) of the Song dynasty. Qian had shown in that section that such "metaphysical" theories of poetry, rather than ignoring technique, anchor themselves firmly in a mastery of craft so subtle as not to allow any of the traces of creation to enter into the realized poetry (48–51).

Qian begins his discourse by outlining Yuan's sophistry in objecting to Yan Yu's use of the process of enlightenment *(wu)* in Chan as a metaphor for poetry. Yuan assumed that by proving the existence of good poetry in China before the coming of Buddhism he could invalidate the analogy. Qian says simply that the intuition characteristic of Chan could have been present long before the coming of the school itself (235–36).[37] He cites as example the *Shishuo Xinyu* [A New Account of Tales of the World], many episodes of which seem to share the spirit of Chan even though that work was completed long before the transmission of Chan teachings to China in the sixth century A.D. (238–39). This argument over the spirit of Chan is but part of a larger one in which Qian is at pains to prove that Yuan Mei, for all his protestations to the contrary, has a theory of poetry that descends directly from the "metaphysical" tradition that begins with Sikong Tu and runs through Yan Yu and Wang Shizhen.[38] Yuan had sought to distance himself from the Chanist orientation of Yan Yu by opposing the idea of *xingling* and substituting "wonderful apprehension" *(miaowu)* as the basis of poetic inspiration. Qian shows the essential similarity and common heritage of the two concepts.

With this point established, Qian moves on to deal with the question of what qualities the poet must bring to poetry. He notes that most critics of Yuan have fixed on such utterances of his as "Poetry is a matter of human feelings. It is enough to take them from close at hand,"[39] and have tried to prove thereby that Yuan values inspiration at the expense of craft. Qian points out that Yuan—like Sikong Tu and Yan Yu before him—has many other passages in which he stresses the importance of learning and craft as necessary preconditions to writing (242). Qian thus shifts the blame for any sloppy theories of poetry that may be said to result from Yuan's theories away from Yuan and onto later critics' misreading of the *Suiyuan Shihua*.

While Qian demonstrates that Yuan does not denigrate learning, it is equally clear from the discussion that the Qing critic displays a marked tendency to oppose learning and inspiration as two entirely different functions of mind. Qian—academic that he is—regrets this, holding that

Unfortunately, we have been born after the ancients, and although we may wish, like Mr. So-and-So, to be completely illiterate, we are but proper people who cannot help remembering things because of the immersion of our eyes and ears [in earlier works of literature]. And these things that we remember are, in fact, sufficient to submerge our sensibilities. . . . But the sensibilities of today all result from the transformation of the half-forgotten learning of an earlier day, which, through habit, has become part of our natures. (243)

The key to the creative transformation of these legacies of the past lies in their artful appropriation by would-be writers (244). Qian's easy solution to what had been for many Chinese writers through history the vexatious problem of overcoming the heritage of a brilliant literature is in line with his condemnation of the idea of genre depletion. It certainly provides appropriate comment on Qian's own creative work, which is extravagantly imbedded with brilliantly turned allusions. Such an open attitude would also have helped Yuan Mei to overcome the problem he sensed when he wrote that "Everything I wish to say of late has invariably already been spoken by someone else."[40]

Related to this question of learning and inspiration is the matter of whether or not poetry can contain "words of moral reason" *(liyou)*, or, in other words, the direct statement of ideas. Yuan says that this is possible[41] (so much for those who regard Yuan as a strict partisan of intuitive expression) and Qian takes him to task for it. Qian argues instead that poetry should not go beyond giving a "sense of ideas" *(liqu)* or a "sense of Chan" *(Chanqu)*. For Qian this is an important distinction, for whereas direct statement is merely bald discourse and not poetry at all, *liqu* is a subtle notion which contains the potential for an evocative poetry that has resonance beyond the simple images it employs. To underline the importance of this distinction, Qian cites numerous examples in each category (265-66). Among others, he lists one line of each type from the poetry of Wang Wei. The example of direct use of Chan language without overtone is "Mountains and rivers within the Buddha's eye; / The universe amid the Dharma body," while the example that gives a "sense of Chan" is "I walk to the place where the waters end; / And sit and watch the time when clouds arise," from the poem "Zhongnan Retreat."[42]

From this, Qian moves on to condemn much Buddhist and Daoist poetry for being mere direct statement, following which he outlines more precisely what he means by "poetic resonance":

In giving words to one's feelings and describing a scene, "inexhaustibility" is what is to be valued. This "inexhaustibility" is like applying a bit of red to a great thicket of green. The author describes one corner and the reader fills in the other three. Seeing this bit of red, one knows that there is in fact a limitless profusion of luxuriant color. . . . There is an insufficiency in the words and a lack of exhaustive description, but there is a deep store of enduring flavor. This is the feeling and the scene. (269)

This is the "meaning beyond words" that is lost when too comprehensive a description is attempted. "Reasoned exposition" *(daoli)* is the exact opposite of this "inexhaustibility": in *daoli* one strives for a generality which will encompass the myriad of phenomena, a single truth to sum up human experience. The very comprehensiveness of such statement precludes the overflow of feeling that is engendered by poetry. The "sense of ideas," however, while lacking the full range of overtone of lyrical poetry, partakes of the spirit of poetry through oblique imagery which leaves the reader to fill in the parts that are unstated. The distinctive thing about *liqu* poetry is that the corners left to be filled in by the reader have to do with general principles, even if the principles themselves rest unuttered. Qian's delineation of *liqu* is in itself somewhat oblique, but the concept would seem to describe aptly the style of *Tan Yi Lu* itself. The avoidance of commonplaces, plentiful use of image and reluctance to make comprehensive theoretical judgments comprise a style which obliges the reader to supply the "other three corners." If this is true for *Tan Yi Lu,* it is even more characteristic of the "familiar style" Qian employs in the essays we shall examine in the next chapter.

Qian goes on to analyze what constitutes poetry that gives a "sense of ideas." In an introductory note he avers that the paradoxes embodied in Buddhist *koan* and *gatha* produce images full of *liqu* and thus potential poetry, but adds that the *koan* itself is too flat a statement to produce the overtones required of poetry (268–69). In order for this raw material to be transformed into poetry, it requires elaboration, something that Chan masters—with their determination to misprize words—were not inclined to attend to (277). This discussion adds the dimension to Qian's theory of poetry that he was clearly groping for in his discussion of *Odes to the Setting Sun* (see above, pp. 20–21): the two errors at the extreme opposite ends of the spectrum—either being overly concerned with the specific (as with Li He) or not investing enough labor into poetic rhetoric—are both related to an ultimate lack of attention to integrating the general and the concrete. In spite of the elaborate and ostentatious form of *Tan Yi Lu,* then, Qian ultimately adheres to an almost Confucian sense of finding the mean in his final notion of what literature is.

Before his summary of this issue Qian expands his disquisition to include ideas from Western poetics within his purview. He comments that Aristotle's idea that "Poetry is something more philosophic and of graver import than history, since its statements are of the nature rather of universals, whereas those of history are singulars,"[43] results in a tendency to neglect particulars and thus veer from poetry. According to Qian, poetry with the "sense of ideas" finds its theoretical justification "only in Hegel [, who] believes that the thing achieves itself through the idea and that the idea is manifest in the thing. The empty and the actual give rise to one another and the identical and the different interpenetrate. Image and idea fuse" (273). The ideal poetry, then, has "the idea in it as salt is in water and as honey is in a flower: the form of it is hidden but the quality is there. There is flavor without trace; its visage is at once manifest and not there; it makes a statement but does not make it" (274).

While this is the ideal, it represents a balance of qualities that is unstable. One can err on the side of either too much idea or too much phenomenon. One of the consequences of too much weight on idea is allegory, which Qian holds to be "not the highest form of literary style. The words are here and the meaning is there, but they are made to sleep in the same bed and to be one. Without notes or a special key, one cannot tell the meaning." Before this admonition, however, Qian mentions, almost as in passing, the difference between allegory in China and the West:

We in China take phenomena to illustrate events. We take [for instance] love between a man and a woman to stand for the proper relationship between rulers and ministers. What illustrates is actual and what is illustrated is also actual. Dante [, however,] uses things to illustrate truths. He uses love between a man and a woman to illustrate the relationship of heaven to mankind. What illustrates is actual but what is illustrated is abstract. One sort of poetry becomes history and the other becomes abstruse. (275)

While Qian does not go into the consequences of these two different types of allegory, the reader can certainly imagine how the Chinese form of event displacing event more readily gives rise to the search for historical instance which Qian objected to in the Qing commentators on Li He. It is also not hard to see how the subjection of literature to the purposes of history places more specific constraints on writing than does the subjection of literature to abstract ideas. In fact, Qian's repeated mention of the ability of Western poetry to treat at once of the universal and the specific, a point he makes most forcefully in his review of *Odes to the Setting Sun,* demonstrates the extent to which he was conscious of this as a limitation on Chinese literature. So while Qian wishes to stick to the mean, the scale for this mean is one which also makes reference to a fundamentally Western ontology.

Tan Yi Lu is a difficult book to sum up, composed of a multitude of parts, with common themes cropping up the more carefully one reads. In it Qian clearly wishes to keep tradition alive, yet he brings in Western ideas that often vary from premodern Chinese poetics. At times he urgently persuades, at others he merely sets out facts. In sum, *Tan Yi Lu* is at once a sober corrective to ideas that Qian feels inhibit the healthy growth of literature and full of lyrical excursions that render many passages perfect examples of literature with the "sense of ideas." The book thus sets the reader the same sort of problem that Geoffrey Hartman has in mind when he asks, "Does the essay, and the literary essay in particular, have a form of its own, a shape or perspective that removes it from the domain of positive knowledge to give it a place beside art, yet without confusing the boundaries of scholarship and art?"[44]

Qian himself, in his introduction to Le Gros Clark's translations, is chary of giving an affirmative answer to such a question. In discussing Sikong Tu's *Shi Pin,* he says that it "is perhaps the earliest piece of 'impressionist' or 'creative criticism' ever written in any language, so quietly ecstatic and so autonomous and self-sufficient, as it were, in its being; but it fails on that very account to become sober and proper criticism."[45] *Tan Yi Lu*'s meticulous attention to detail and evidence, along with its copious documentation, avoid any "autonomous self-sufficiency" which would hinder it from being considered "sober and proper criticism."

But at the same time, the work is nothing if not "creative criticism."

Perhaps an explanation for these paradoxes lies in Qian's awareness of the cultural alienation of modern China: the iconoclastic milieu created by the May Fourth movement endangered the Chinese literary heritage. But while aware of the need to conserve, Qian was also mindful of the need for renewal. He hoped that what was good in the old literature could be separated from limitations imposed by ideological features of the tradition that could now be dispensed with. While this task sounds easy in theory, it in fact stymied most literary men in modern China. The sensitivity of Qian's critiques illustrates his consciousness of its extraordinary complexity. He also, of course, devoutly wished to avoid seeking that spurious legitimacy in tradition that he condemned so harshly in his essay on poetry and painting. The central paradox, then, lies in his sense of the need for both continuity and discontinuity. He chose a difficult style, one which could, in Hartman's words, "expose virtues and weaknesses, strong points and failings together," as well as "frighten" its readers "by opening a breach—or the possibility of transvaluation—in almost every received value."[46] As a result, *Tan Yi Lu* is such a work as Hartman has in mind when he says that

literary commentary may cross the line and become as demanding as literature; it is an unpredictable and unstable "genre" that cannot be subordinated, a priori, to its referential or commentary function. . . . The perspectival power of criticism, its strength of recontextualization, must be such that the critical essay should not be considered a supplement to something else. (265)

For all Qian's virtuosity as a critic and Hartman's claims for the critical essay, however, it is useful to keep in mind Northrop Frye's injunction about literary commentary:

Commentary . . . is allegorization and any great work of literature may carry an infinite amount of commentary. . . . Commentary which has no sense of the archetypal shape of literature as a whole, then, continues the tradition of allegorized myth and inherits its characteristics of brilliance, ingenuity and futility."[47]

While Frye is clearly grinding his pet axe here, this comment does help dispel the fashionable notion that literary criticism is the equal of literature. *Tan Yi Lu*, then—Hartman notwithstanding—has its limitations as a vehicle for sustaining the Chinese literary tradition. It is perhaps for this reason that Qian admitted in 1979 that he had always wished to be a satirical novelist more than anything else: Chinese literature could only continue through the creation of literary works. It is his efforts in this sphere that will be the subject of the remainder of this study.

Chapter Four
The Essays

Initial reading of the informal essays that Qian Zhongshu wrote in the late 1930s leaves the reader uncertain about their intent. There is a shrinking from resolution in the mélange of solemnity and frivolity that marks both their content and their tone. So ambiguous are these writings that it becomes possible to gain a fix on them only by setting them in the broad context of the development of modern Chinese vernacular prose. When looked at from this perspective, the shifting content becomes less important than an underlying concern with a form involving conscious and unconscious calculation about the relationship of writing to thought process.

Prose Old and New

As the discussion in *Tan Yi Lu* about the problems of language should have made clear, prose style has always been of great import for Chinese scholars. Many of the principal events in Chinese intellectual history, such as the Tang restoration of "ancient-style" prose, the iconoclasm of the late Ming and the Tongcheng school of the Qing, centered around writing reform. The accelerating decline of the state and its ideology in the first two decades of the twentieth century thus naturally pushed prose style once again to the forefront of intellectual concern. As the political crisis deepened, scholars turned increasingly from the traditional focus on reconciling the needs to give expression to contemporary reality and to employ forms consonant with Confucian morality, to consider the possibility of a more general insufficiency residing within the norms of the literary language itself. Hundreds of years of tight control over the means of expression began to appear to have created a written language that was far from adequate to the needs of a more complex time. It was for this reason that the intellectual impetus behind the May Fourth movement was a radical call to replace the standard literary language, based almost entirely on classical Chinese, with a vernacular written language for which the possibilities of expository expression were as yet largely unexplored.

The May Fourth reformers diagnosed the problems with the literary language as residing in the tendency of those who wrote it to copy already established styles and to give precedence to form over content. Hu Shi's (1891–1962) famous "Eight Don'ts" for writing comprise a negative list of the shortcomings that imitation and blind adherence to convention brought about:

1. Don't write words without content.
2. Don't write mournfully without a real complaint.
3. Don't use allusions.
4. Don't use set phrases and clichés.
5. Don't use balanced phrasing—in prose discard parallelism, in poetry discard regulation.
6. Don't write ungrammatically.
7. Don't imitate the ancients.
8. Don't avoid colloquial expression.[1]

Numbers three, four, seven, and eight all refer to Hu's wish to have writers break away from stale semantic usage. Number five, however, is a matter of syntax: the ordering of words and phrases that allowed the insincerity and lack of substance addressed by the first two items on the agenda.

Most writers of the period saw balanced phrasing as ubiquitous in the literary language and—probably because of its association with the despised "eight-legged" essay—this parallelism was regarded as the central defect of the classical style. Zhou Zuoren goes even farther than this in an essay on *bagu wen* appended to *The Origins of the New Chinese Literature*. He sees the Chinese love for empty mesmerizing rhythms, represented by the "eight-legged" essay, as "always having been the crystallization of

Chinese literature—no, one can be more brave and say that it is the crystallization of Chinese culture."[2] It is no wonder that Zhou finds parallelism at the heart of all the various schools of Qing dynasty prose and the direct cause of the literary revolution that began in 1917. While noting the withering away of *bagu* per se after the abolition of the civil service examination system in 1905, Zhou warns of its continuing recrudescence even in the new vernacular styles created after 1920. The prevalence of such terms as *"Yang bagu"* (foreign *bagu*) after May Fourth lends credence to his fears: the habits engendered by traditional forms lived on long after the supposedly uncontaminated vernacular had come into general use.

Fear of being unconsciously trapped into seductive old patterns of rhetoric lay behind the self-proclaimed minimality of the narrative style of Zhou's brother, Lu Xun:

I did my best to avoid all wordiness. If I felt I had made my meaning sufficiently clear, I was glad not to have any extraneous backgrounding. . . . Convinced that such methods suited my purpose, I did not indulge in irrelevant details and kept the dialogue down to a minimum.[3]

Modern reformers had, however, found alternatives to ritual imitation within the literary language itself. Zhou Zuoren so extravagantly admired the writers of the late Ming Gongan school precisely because of their abundantly expressed disdain for all sorts of literary archaism and their apparent disposition to obey Hu Shi's injunctions some three hundred years before the fact.[4] But for all the Gongan advocacy of freshness and fluidity, their careful steering away from allusion and complexity had created a problem in its own right, a sterility of effect—something that was vexing the new vernacular as well. As Zhou says of the Gongan school:

Their compositions were too empty and facile, clear without being deep. As with a pool of water, it obviously does not do for it to be too muddied, but if it is so clear that the eye can see straight to the bottom, and all the plants and fishes in it can be sharply discerned, there is no interest in it.[5]

Attitudes toward the literary language in the May Fourth period thus seem to harbor an unresolvable contradiction: classical prose is hobbled by a rhetorical baggage that draws attention to itself rather than the thing being described: but if the rhetoric is abandoned altogether, the style that remains is so lacking in resonance as to satisfy no one. The problem is so deeply rooted that the May Fourth classical/vernacular conflict was in a sense only the latest manifestation of an underlying struggle that had been going on for hundreds of years between, on the one hand, pattern and allusion and, on the other, lack of adornment. The continuity is marked by the frequency with which critics added the censorious term *bagu* to new sorts of vernacular writing as well as by the insipidness of much of the vernacular writing of the years following 1917—notably the poetic efforts of Hu Shi. Zhou Zuoren, writing in 1936, laments this impasse. He is puzzled as to why it should exist, but says that it results, "if not in a new type of vulgar *bagu*, then a preachiness in the old foreign manner."[6] The foreignness he mentions is what writers casting about for the clear expository style that the Chinese vernacular lacked seized upon. In trying to avoid being captured by the past, many writers turned to imitation of European styles, a fact which is itself testimony to the hollowness of the new vernacular; the unacceptability of such borrowing to all sides of the literary and political spectrum is illustrated by the universal disapproval it encountered.[7]

The phenomenon of stylistic reform is not unique to Chinese literary history: the European "Baroque" revolt of the early seventeenth century against the Latin Ciceronian prose of the Renaissance was similar. As Montaigne wrote in his "Consideration upon Cicero," "I know well that when I hear someone dwell on the language of these [i.e., Montaigne's own] essays, I would rather he said nothing. This is not so much to extol the style as to depreciate the sense. . . . Fie on the eloquence that leaves us craving itself, not things!"[8] European writers of that time, however, in trying to demonstrate the way to a new vernacular prose, were able to draw extensively on their literary tradition, if only to turn it on its head. As Rosalie Colie says of Robert

Burton: "With his striking independence in the use of sources, Burton demonstrates the typical humanist disregard of the contextual demands of these sources, pillaging for his own purposes, to suit himself, to buttress his argument or to illustrate his point, however he chose to do so."[9] In other words, Western literary reformers had license that traditional Chinese prose reformers like the Gongan group apparently lacked to subvert the prevailing style by using it against itself—ironically employing older terms of the language to show how they failed in their referential function. As Pascal wrote: *"La vraie eloquence se moque de l'eloquence."*[10]

The ultimate reason behind this difference in flexibility toward the past probably lay in divergent ontologies of prose. As the discussion of different types of allegory in *Tan Yi Lu* demonstrates, Western metaphysics had posited a real, if transcendental, otherness of which writing was no more than the signature; but in China writing was both signature *and* essential portion of the moral holism to which it gave expression.[11] In the West, where writing was amenable to being regarded as a tool which could be tinkered with, it was possible to gain an independent perspective over the medium. In China, however, writing was part and parcel of what it signified and it was consequently not easy to find leverage with which to attack the trustworthiness of the medium itself. It was thus only after the overthrow of the Confucian world-view in the May Fourth period that drastic stylistic reform became even a theoretical possibility.

The few modern Chinese writers who clearly saw the paradox of the choices with which they were faced and did not despair took action in a manner remarkably similar to that of those Europeans who had sought to establish the legitimacy of their vernacular languages in the early 1600s. Foremost among these was Lu Xun. For all his harping upon minimality, his style is often marked by the allusions, tropes and diction of classical prose; but he suffused this usage with a deliberate irony calculated to demonstrate the hollowness of the literary language. Some of the clearest examples of this method appear in the story "Kong Yiji." To begin with, the eponymous protagonist's name itself is taken from a children's calligraphic copy book, thus hinting at the arbitrary nature of language use; as the story develops, a central tension is the constant play on the differences between the literary and the ordinary languages. Having the literary language housed in such a wretched vehicle as the hypocritical Kong pointedly shows the lack of any referential value for the classical terminology. When, for instance, his fellow drinkers accuse him of stealing *(tou)* books, he replies that he has "purloined" *(qie)* them, an affair of "men of letters" and thus not to be considered stealing.[12] Similarly, he is always ready with his "mouthful of archaisms" to utter a classical homily that, rather than producing its intended effect, does nothing but provoke laughter.

It is in his essays, however, that Lu Xun most clearly undermines tradition. In his famous work "On Deferring 'Fair Play,' " he calls the bluff of those who sought to return to traditional values by invoking the mottoes concerning the return to the Golden Age and pushing on them to reveal the absolute lack of sense behind such vague exhortations. The resulting contrast with anyone's perception of reality starkly illuminates the lack of substance in the sacred images:

Some Chinese believe in traditional Chinese medicine, and both types of doctors can now be found in our larger towns, so that patients may take their choice. I thoroughly approve of this. If this were applied more generally, I am sure there would be fewer complaints, and perhaps we could even secure peace and prosperity. For instance, the usual form of greeting now is to bow; but if anyone disapproves of this, he can kowtow instead. The new penal code has no punishment by bastinado; but if anyone approves of corporal punishment, when he breaks the law he can have his bottom specially spanked. Bowls, chopsticks, and cooked food are the custom today; but if anyone hankers after the times before Suiren Shi, he can eat raw meat. We can also build several thousand thatched huts, and move all those fine gentlemen who so admire the age of Yao and Shun out of their big houses to live there; while those who oppose material civilization should certainly not be compelled to travel in cars. When this is done, there will really be a situation in which "those who seek benevolence will achieve benevolence; what will they have to complain of?" And our ears will be left in peace.[13]

The structure of this passage contributes significantly to its general purpose: beginning with a perfectly acceptable premise about medicine, Lu Xun builds a series of parallel phrases which becomes even more outrageous. By constructing this series of traditional homilies in traditional parallel style, he contrives to discredit both conventional ideas and the form in which they are cast. The circuit of self-reflecting ideas and style is demolished by overloading the structure so that it falls of its own weight.

Prose segments in Lu Xun's writing, moreover, tend to be short: seldom does an essay develop a specific argument in a systematic way over an extended space. Each paragraph stands as a unit with only tenuous links to the next. The essay under consideration, for example, switches back and forth between the "beating dogs in the water" image and the contemporary situations to which it refers without apparent concern for logical development. Most of his essays, in fact, especially the later ones, are so short as to preclude the question of logical development. This brevity, coupled with Lu Xun's aversion to "backgrounding" imply a clear mistrust of language. The desire to write in short periods was also characteristic of the European reformers and is evidence of a similar concern with what Stanley Fish calls "a method of communication which neutralizes the errors the understanding is prone to. . . ." Thus, "In place of an 'artificial method' with full and articulated divisions, Bacon recommends 'short and scattered sentences not linked together,' aphorisms which will not give the impression that 'they pretend or profess to embrace the entire art.' "[14]

In the small group of prose reformers conscious of the defects of traditional style and its temptations to the modern writer, Lu Xun's method is widespread. Later critics have labelled this the "Lu Xun style" and have attempted to show how it derived from the master. It would appear, however, to have had a broader origin as part of the movement against "new *bagu,*" in which a variety of writers participated who seem to have had in common only a persistently critical outlook on contemporary patterns of thought and society's failure to look at its hypocrisies full on.[15]

The Essays

This style's characteristically short, nonsequential development and ironic highlighting of classical allusion did not escape the attention of contemporary critics. Li Jianwu points out these qualities in the prose of the writer Fei Ming and brings up as well the crucial factor of audience response. Li describes the lack of internal links in Fei Ming's prose thus:

He has the longest gaps between sentence and sentence. The length of these gaps makes one pause to consider. . . . Mr. Fei Ming's gaps are always the result of his sentences lacking clear "bridges" between them. Because of this, you can apprehend his mode of writing. He begins from the concept and each concept congeals into a crystallized sentence. [You], the reader cannot help resting here at each point, because you have been provided with an overly long train of thought.[16]

This passage is reminiscent of Fish's summary of Bacon's style, pointing out Fei Ming's probable intention of not allowing the reader to be swept along by standardized and automatic trains of thought. Li also discusses Fei Ming's relative lack of popularity:

Mr. Fei Ming's method of expression is so new and so unique that it precludes reception by many easy readers. Let us boil down the issue to inspect it. Mr. Fei Ming likes to use allusions, no matter whether the source is poetry, lyric, drama or the essay. When he uses them, however, he never fails to extend their significance or to offer up a new meaning. And the result is that his use of allusion becomes a barrier to the ordinary reader. . . . No matter what, most people regard it [i.e., his use of allusion] as obscure; sometimes it is the exact opposite [of its original sense]. But this is a guiding light to the minority. (193)

This fully brings out the reader's side of the experience of such essays: he or she is expected to work harder to apprehend what is being conveyed. The old smoothness of an ingrained rhetoric common to both reader and writer is purposefully ruffled. In the new style, the reader is forced to think things through anew and reconstruct the ultimate sense of each essay for himself. This style, then, was largely negative—the old conventions had to be broken down before positive synthesis and construction of new ideas, immune from the dangers of slipping into old traces, could be safely undertaken.

"Discussing Friendship"

The "baroque style" in modern Chinese is nowhere as well represented as in Qian Zhongshu's occasional essays. Of the eleven that I have seen, ten are contained in the collection *Xie zai Rensheng Bianshang,* which translates, somewhat awkwardly, as *Written on the Margin of Life*. The book was published in Shanghai in 1941 with a preface dated February [19]39. As there are a few references to the war and to the "interior" in the essays, it is probable that they were written while the author was in Yunnan during the early years of the war. The first piece, "Mogui Ye Fang Qian Zhongshu Xiansheng" [Satan Pays an Evening Visit to Mr. Qian Zhongshu], is narrative representation, containing a storyteller and a story and, as such, will be discussed in the next chapter. The essay not collected in the book, entitled "Tan Jiaoyou" [Discussing Friendship], was published in the first issue of Zhu Guangqian's *Wenxue Zazhi* [Literature Magazine] in May 1937; it was written in January 1937, during the second of Qian's two years at Oxford. This earlier essay contains important elements of the critical style discussed above, but it is twice as long and lacks the fine tautness and mordant punch of the pieces published during the war.

The first paragraph of "Discussing Friendship," though, is characteristic of all the essays. It begins, "If love is a necessity of life, then friendship can only be considered a type of luxury."[17] The rest of the paragraph goes on to give various facets and illustrations of this truth: a luxury is more to be valued than a necessity, thus it is with friendship and love. This sort of statement and elaboration is characteristic of Qian's essay style; it fits almost exactly the description of the *stile coupé* of seventeenth-century European writing, which Morris Croll describes in his well-known article "The Baroque Style in Prose":

The first member [of a period], therefore, exhausts the mere fact of the idea; logically there is nothing more to say. But it does not exhaust its imaginative truth or the energy of its conception. It is followed, therefore, by other members, each with a new tone or emphasis, each expressing a new apprehension of the truth expressed in the first. We may describe the progress of a curt period, therefore, as a series of imaginative moments occurring in a logical pause or suspension. Or—to be less obscure—we may compare it with successive flashes of a jewel or prism as it is turned about on its axis and takes the light in different ways.[18]

"Discussing Friendship" 's prose is also marked by parallelism, such as: "In lovers although one wants new ones to maintain interest, in friends one still considers old ones best" (187–88). Furthermore, the last sentence of the paragraph composes a trope that is constantly to reappear: after steadfastly holding to the superiority of friends over lovers through so many sentences, Qian summarizes by saying, "This, of course, cannot be generalized—it depends on what sort of friends you have" (188). This sort of paradoxical construction is also characteristic of seventeenth-century European prose; as Fish analyzes a similar construction of Bacon's:

if anything is being clarified here, it is the extent to which the confidently proffered pronouncement of the first sentence does not hold up under close scrutiny; and, moreover, the reader's experience of that clarification is somewhat chastening, since it involves the debunking of something he had accepted without question.[19]

This device, which I shall call the *chedan fa* ("nonsense" or "making light" method, so called because Qian the fictional narrator often has one of his characters end a tense scene by *chedan,* or making a joke out of the situation), is the only sure marker of a transition in the essays. It signals not a logical transition within a developing theme, but simply the wrapping-up of one discussion so that a new one can be broached. It often equilibrates the two contrasting features of one issue, in mimicry of the traditional essay. But unlike the traditional essay, the equilibration in this case is purely negative: the two features are equated only in the sense that neither is left standing.

The second paragraph opens with three sentences which perform in miniature the same undermining function as the whole first paragraph: "The Western proverb which goes 'a friend in need is a friend indeed' is unavoidably shallow. When we are most in need is when we least need friends. If a friend has money, we need his money; if a friend has rice, what we lack is his rice." Here, instead of waiting until the end of the paragraph to deny the validity of the commonplace, Qian shocks us out of our belief in the predicate of the first sentence. He then begins to unveil his real message, which is that we should not confuse utilitarian motives with genuine friendship. When we are in need, "we may perhaps need real friends, but what we really need is not friends." Thus only after the initial denial of convention can Qian bring us to any affirmation—only when the reader has been forced to confront how standard practice consists of partial truths is he allowed to see the genuine truth behind it. Qian then proceeds for almost a page to bring out the problematics of this initial contrast between utility and friendship. The prose is full of parallel constructions and traditional sayings; as could be expected from the first use of the proverb, the intention in using these traditional elements is most often to show how they do not do justice to reality. For example, in a sentence illustrating the difficulty of not allowing utility to stand in the way of friendship when we are hard up, Qian writes:

With both sleeves full of pure air, with a mouth gulping pure water, to say that one can listen intently to a good friend's pure talk, forgetting our hunger and thirst, even gentlemen so pure as to completely lack human qualities will not necessarily be able to endure such pure misery. (188)

The set of parallel sayings in the first part of this sentence, all predicated upon the word "pure" *(qing)*, with its corresponding noble associations, is brought crashing down by the final phrase's doubt over whether such "pure" misery can be endured. The final *qing* abruptly reverses the sense of the period and stirs the reader to doubt the whole structure of easily consumed cliché which preceded it. Furthermore, even the most inveterate devotee of *bagu* style will have begun to squirm under the constant iteration of the key word long before the coming of the final and definitely ironic *qing*. This is a fine example of the overplaying of a traditional device to the point where attention is drawn to structure and its inherent defects.

The discursive section on the difficulties of friendship is brought to an end by another *chedan* paradox. Qian apparently makes the definitive statement on the subject by writing that "Friendship in times of trouble is worth the least money of all," but he immediately follows this phrase with a dash and adds, "No, it is most susceptible to being gauged by monetary value!" (189), which propels the reader straight back into a state of confusion. Is friendship a matter of utility after all? Or not? Is Qian being ironic in some new way? This further sapping of reader confidence is given immediacy by the author's device of seeming to reverse his field right before our eyes—of giving us the impression that Qian is thinking directly on the page before us. This trick is common in his other writings as well, and is yet one more characteristic that is also common to the "baroque style." As Croll puts it:

[Sir Henry] Wotton [the author of the passage Croll is discussing] has deliberately avoided the processes of mental revision to express his idea when it is nearer the point of origin in his mind. We must stop for a moment on the word deliberately. . . . [E]ven their [i.e., Wotton and other writers who employ the same device] extravagances are purposive, and express a creed that is at the same time philosophical and artistic. Their purpose was to portray, not a thought, but a mind thinking, or, in Pascal's words, *la peinture de la pensée*. They knew that an idea separated from the act of experiencing it is not the idea that was experienced. The order of its conception in the mind is a necessary part of its truth; and unless it can be conveyed to another mind in something of the form of its occurrence, either it has changed into some other idea or it has ceased to be an idea, to have any existence whatever except a verbal one.[20]

This sense of immediacy is perhaps one of the things to which Qian was referring in the distinction between "familiar" and "formal" prose set out in Chapter 2.

The transition that follows is not to a new area of discussion, but to a long passage in which he invokes literary authority for the problem he has just set out. While trotting out various sources which complain about the infidelity of friends, he introduces one of the themes that is to recur throughout his writings, that of the necessity of looking at things from more sides than just the one of personal interest. In a sense this has been foreshadowed in his initial discussion of luxury and necessity. "Luxuries," in which he seems to include all those things which separate the human from the animal, also encompass the ability to transcend absolute selfishness. From this point, Qian moves from the "material" side of friendship to the "spiritual." In the following discussion Qian maintains the basic dichotomy between utilitarian "friends" (in this case, "friends that can help you"—the *yiyou* of Confucius[21]) and the friends one makes without selfish motives; Qian builds a case for the general irksomeness of such *yiyou* and proceeds to show how such "beneficial" friends may not be so beneficial after all.

The essay eventually goes on to deal with aspects of knowledge in general (in the context of enumerating the supposed good points of *yiyou*) and comes to the fairly conventional conclusion that the amount of knowledge one possesses per se is less important than the capacity to create more. That was, he says, the traditional view. But the way in which Qian goes on to develop this point is illustrative of an important feature of his prose style. After stating the traditional opinion on the matter, he says:

But the situation now is not at all the same. *Au courant* scholars no longer need a mind [*xin*]; a few drawers and several hundred blank cards, classified in categories, will comprise an index enabling them to find what they need without forcing their brains to go through the effort of memorization. As long as the drawers are full, what does it matter if the mind is empty? If one begins by substituting drawers for brains, as time passes and things transform with use, the brain becomes a bit wooden like the material comprising the drawer. I should dare to predict, then, that such present-day terms of abuse as blockhead and woodenhead will become the most respected appellations of scholars, and the term "unvarnished learning" [*pu xue*] will take on fresh meaning. (194)

Aside from being a massive *chedan*, which serves to take the reader away from the unpleasant realm of utilitarian considerations, this paragraph develops in a way which sheds some light on general features of Qian's informal prose. The image develops with a substitution of the word "drawer" for the word "mind," rather than as an organically connected discourse concerned with the various qualities causatively associated with the notion of mind, such as what it performs, how it does so, and what the implications of these processes are. The sudden leap effected by this replacement of one quality by another in the same syntactic position cuts off the possibility of logical development.

From this point on, however, "Discussing Friendship" ceases to be ironic and becomes a positive paean to the glories of friendship and to his own friends. The great contrasts between luxury and necessity and utility and unselfishness are left behind, and the reader is finally allowed to relax without further challenge to his conventional sensibilities. A certain residual discontent remains, but it is contextual—Qian's unhappiness with his isolation in England—rather than connected with the problematics of the categories under discussion themselves. Such a letting-down of guard is seldom found in Qian's other creative texts. This thematic loosening of attitude is matched by the structure of the essay: it is about twice as long as the essays in *Margin,* the examples adduced for each category of behavior go on past the point of marginal utility, and the various digressions often have little to do with the overall impact of the work. In his later essays, the asperity of style tallies perfectly with the asperity of theme.

The "Marginalia"

Qian sets the theme and explains the title of *Margin* in a short preface which he appends to the book. After reporting that he has "heard that human life is a large book," he says that if that be true, then "the great majority of us authors can only be considered critics, possessing the talent of the critic to compile a great stack of opinions without having read many pages." But he goes on to describe a type of author who is too lazy to write proper "criticism," contenting himself instead, when the occasion demands, with "jotting a few words in the margin of the text."

These jottings are not meant to be conclusive, so if they contain contradiction and exaggeration, it is of no real consequence: "At any rate, it is only an amusement, unlike [the task] of the 'critics' who take upon themselves the great missions of leading and instructing their readers. Who has the patience to do such things?"[22] Furthermore, the "book of life" is so large that it is not easy to read through; thus "there will even be a considerable number of blanks among the marginalia" (ii). Together, these statements resemble nothing so much as Bacon's disclaiming of holistic intent cited above. Qian is, in fact, being more than a little coy; he is informing the reader that he can relax with the text and not worry about being put through a rigorous course of instruction—attempting, in other words, to disarm him. To the extent that this effort is successful, the sharp and intricate points made in the essays to come will hit even harder. The preface contains only the first of innumerable false expectations implanted in the book.

Aside from the first essay, which is really a story, *Margin* contains nine pieces of writing. Although none of them lacks its serious sides, gravity of subject matter tends to increase toward the end of the book. Rather than discuss each essay piecemeal and incompletely, I shall deal extensively with only one, the sixth of the nine, entitled "Tan Jiaoxun" [Discussing Instruction]. At the end of each paragraph translated, appropriate commentary will be appended; analogous features in other essays will be discussed as well. Although "Instruction" is somewhat more dour and pointed than most of the other pieces, it contains all the significant tropes present in the collection as a whole. Since Qian had, as will presently become obvious, a set of rhetorical purposes in mind in composing the collection, it is perhaps most sensible to choose an essay for discussion where these purposes stand out particularly clearly. "Instruction" is to be found on pages 41–47 of the Hong Kong reprint edition of *Margin*.

[1] One dislikes dirt, so one expresses a love of cleanliness; because of this, people who are fanatical about cleanliness would rather not bathe than use the bathing equipment of others. [2] The difference between dirt and cleanliness as a result becomes the distinction between oneself

and others. [3] Those who consider themselves clean always suspect others of being unkempt; this is carried to the point that even if the admission is made that one is dirty, it is still easier to accept than a clean neighbor; a sweat-covered body and foul-smelling breath are preferable to borrowing another's toothbrush or washcloth. [4] Of course, aside from those who are willing to make an exception in the case of a lover, one is also completely unwilling to extend one's own toothbrushes and washcloths to friends. [5] Looked at this way, we do not love cleanliness, we rather only love ourselves. [6] The saying "the clean body loves itself" contains a good deal of psychological insight. [7] To speak frankly, the world's distinctions between right and wrong, good and evil, heterodoxy and orthodoxy and so on are nothing more than the distinction between self and other, just like bodily cleanliness and filth. [8] If one wishes to be a good person, therefore, one must first always declare the world's other people all to be bad eggs; to become a moral exemplar, then, first square the countenance and proclaim how others are not moral exemplars or are fraudulent moral exemplars. [9] Having written this, we cannot help thinking of the female spirit's reply to the fox fairy: "You say I'm not a person, but just what sort of person are you?"

This paragraph ends with a characteristic *chedan,* but rather than being a digression like the example from the end of "Discussing Friendship," it is a bit of lightening that refers directly to the main theme of the paragraph. The first sentence carries us quickly from the commonplace of the first phrase on to the slightly less acceptable truth of the second sentence, without giving us pause to examine whether or not the train of thought is legitimate. In fact, the "because of this" *(yinci)* which links the truism about love for cleanliness to the eventual conclusion of selfishness is fraudulent: the *yinci* leaps a logical chasm that takes us from truism to debatable idiosyncracy. As a result, Qian subtly undermines the seeming certainty of the first phrase and the reader is left wallowing in relativism.[23] This is also the method used in "Discussing Friendship's" second paragraph, where he saps the aphorism "a friend in need. . . ." The process in the present essay, however, is more subtle, since the author refrains from direct comment on the proposition's validity; the negation is accomplished instead by the abruptness of the progression itself.

After the shocking rapidity of the transformation in the first two sentences, however, Qian slows the pace by adducing the several illustrations that the only difference between cleanliness and filth is a subjective one; the reader is lulled into trusting the author once again.

Toward the end of this section, however, in the seventh sentence, the chain of thought explodes again when Qian extends his reference from the relatively insignificant matter of cleanliness to—by implication at least—every human value: those who seek to establish values are merely being more selfish than others. This shocking assertion fits into the complex of themes which is Qian's constant concern: the need to transcend selfishness, to reexamine conventional views with their circular logic and to take steps toward the truly human only after painful examination of how much of people's behavior is truly bestial.

Structurally, Qian's intention of forcing rigorous examination of the commonplace requires him to break down configurations of meaning as he builds them up. The points at which he backs off and plays to reader expectation are merely illusions necessary to orient the reader in the essentially hostile territory of the marginalia. For, as Wolfgang Iser says:

Without the formation of illusions, the unfamiliar world of the text would remain unfamiliar; through the illusions, the experience offered by the text becomes accessible to us, for it is only the illusion, on its different levels of consistency, that makes the experience "readable." If we cannot find (or impose) this consistency, sooner or later we will put the text down.[24]

But just as the reader begins to feel comfortable, Qian again cuts the ground away, revealing the emptiness of yet another area of conventional wisdom. To the extent that the reader was momentarily lulled, however, the undermining process is that much more effective.

With the eighth sentence we finally come to the announced topic of the essay: the issue of moral instruction. The introduction of the real matter to be discussed some time after the opening is typical of Qian's essays and fiction.[25] This style of beginning with anecdote or exposition only tangentially related to the main business is reminiscent of the introductory material in traditional Chinese fiction and drama; it serves to immerse the reader in a particular mood without going through the logical or narrative process of setting it.

Paragraph two:

[1] I often wonder why there are so many people in the world who pump up their courage to serve as obligatory advisors to mankind, who publish essays every day to instruct mankind. [2] *That animal called man* [English in the original], although—contrary to what one would expect—not susceptible to complete extinction, has a few among its number who have achieved self-mastery and can save others. [3] I further wonder, with so many people instructing it, why mankind has not reformed. [4] This, of course, is like asking: since the world has so many practicing doctors of benevolent heart and clever device, why is mankind still diseased? [5] Doctors, however, although they treat illness, wish at the same time for people to be ill; in administering bitter medicine and extracting burning fees, doctors save their own lives while saving the lives of others: if there were no sick people devouring medicine, doctors would not be able to devour food. [6] Having moral advisors without human nature changing, therefore, is nothing really extraordinary; the incapacity of human nature to reform itself yet still having people take up the burden of instruction is, on the other hand, something to give one pause. [7] At any rate, men are not amenable to teaching; instructional essays, although without any real use in the world or in human hearts, are always needed, just as when we become ill we have to see the doctor and take medicine, even if the illness is not cured as a result. [8] If mankind could really improve itself, it would not need to receive any more instruction; would it not, then, have been a waste that so many people have been killed? [9] To move from the responsibilities of human life to the attitudes of the critic, if the writing of essay after essay of straightforwardly preachy prose creates things of little value, neither does paper or ink cost very much. [10] With the bridge of human life, as for Dante, already half passed over, a *Divine Comedy,* however, not even begun; for falling in love or going to war it would seem a bit late; for deserting the world and becoming a monk, it would seem a bit early; if thinking of creating something, it would seem that talent is exhausted; if thinking of study,

preparation is regretfully lacking—at such a time if he did not write missionary-style essays, what would you have him do?

With the "truth" that all distinctions are merely selfish ones already established in the first paragraph, the first sentence of the second paragraph follows naturally. The third sentence, however, seems at first glance to reopen the question, but the subsequent sentences show it just to be a rhetorical question, meant to highlight the futility of the effort being described. Sentences four through seven illustrate the conclusion that instruction is just an outgrowth of selfishness by drawing invidious comparisons with a presumptively corrupt medical profession. It is not until sentence seven, however, that Qian flatly states that mankind cannot be instructed; he even makes that utterance seem more offhand by tossing in a casual "at any rate" *(fanzheng)*. Sentences two and eight do not seem to fit into the typical form of exposition: the conjunction "contrary to what one would expect" *(juran)* in sentence two has no connection with anything that has been set up as an expectation, and the statement about the waste of killing people seems gratuitous. The explanation is probably that these are two of the few references in the essays to the ongoing war:[26] the implication is that war is the result of misapplied efforts at reform of the human race. Neither sentence, however, is integrated into the text, perhaps indicating an inability or unwillingness to approach the subject directly. (All of his creative works, in fact, were written during the war and steer clear of confronting its moral implications head on—something on which Qian commented in 1979—see below, p. 118). Sentence ten shifts to a new image so abruptly and impersonally that the reader at first does not know exactly what is happening or to whom. The mood similarly seems to shift—the solemnity of Dante's life crisis, one of the great images in literature, appears to be impelling us toward seriousness. It is only with the last two phrases that Qian "makes light" of the proceedings and signals to us that there is to be a transition. The very length of the sentence has, however, left us in suspense as long as possible.

The third paragraph treats the notion of moral instruction as the particular province of the middle-aged. The paragraph is in baroque form: initial statement followed by a multitude of illustrations. Paragraph four continues:

[1] There is a type of person whose financial principle is to borrow and not pay back; there is, therefore, a type of person whose moral principle is simply to instruct others without having any morals himself. [2] The saying in the classics that the "good person" is he who "can accept all instruction" is unavoidably too shallow. [3] The really good person bestows and does not accept, he only permits himself to instruct others and is never willing to accept the instruction of others: this is the so-called spirit of sacrifice. [4] Of course, moving from an artistic view of life to a moral one can be said to be the product of a new age of human life. [5] But the beginning of each new age is simultaneously the ending of an old one. [6] For example, in the eyes of the employed, breakfast is today's beginning: when one has eaten one's fill work may begin; but from the viewpoint of those of the leisured class who stay up all night playing cards or dancing until morning, breakfast is the conclusion of last night: eating one's fill aids sleep. [7] The birth of moral instruction thus may just be the death of creativity. [8] In saying this, I have absolutely no intention of praising or condemning; [I] regard one thing as being as important as the other, because the relative values of moral instruction and creativity are decided by each person. [9] Even I myself do not regard creativity as more precious than moral instruction. [10] Some people's literary creations are nothing but preaching with a facade, which is inferior to simply coming out crisply with the moral; on the other hand, some people's morality is something produced from nothing, taking the false for the true, and thus can be considered a creation along with poetry, history, rumors and lies.

This paragraph moves the essay into high-level irony: the last sentence's ostensible and real meanings are completely at odds. The rest of the essay continues in this mode. This irony is attained by means of various devices; one is the false syllogism of the first sentence. As in many other of Qian's assertions, the truth of the existence of people who only borrow and never pay back is debatable at best, but it is elevated to undeserved universality by the term "financial principle," which strongly implies a constant rule. And even if it were true, the "therefore" which connects it with its presumed equivalent in the moral sphere is a case of random substitution rather than the result of a logical construct.

The establishment of these two "principles," in turn, allows the overturning of a more established notion of what a "good person" really is: the specious reasoning of the first sentence, once allowed, enables the speciousness of the second and third to get through. This is all done very rapidly, with characteristic short phrasing, which carries the reader breathlessly through the illogic. The end of the third sentence even adds a further "proof," by introducing another "good" in the same category: "the spirit of sacrifice."

Sentence four reaches back into the previous paragraph to borrow the concept of morality as being *the* replacement for creativity, this in spite of the fact that it had originally been listed as but one of four options to account for a predilection for instructing. The "of course" glosses over this fact and makes it seem as if this proposition were almost axiomatic. After an illustration, the seventh sentence finally comes out with a bold statement of what has presumably long been established, a procedure similar to one that occurs in the second paragraph. This being the third statement of the principle, the reader is meant to be won over by the simple force of its iteration rather than by the presentation of any evidence to support the view. Sentences eight and nine move on to pious disavowal of a personal interest in the issue, thereby— temporarily at least—increasing the reader's confidence in the author's judgment.

The beginning of the tenth sentence represents a continuation of the author's backpedaling: after having posited, with some care, the distinction between morality and creativity, he attempted to show the justness of his observation by stepping back from his personal bias; in the next step back, however, he admits that sometimes, in fact, moralizing and creativity are even reversed, a progress in the analysis that leads us in a circle back to where we started. The final phrase takes the last step in undermining Qian's case by calling false morality as creative as "poetry, history, rumors and lies." Richard Ohmann has recognized a similar process in the writing of George Bernard Shaw; he notes that the second term in one of Shaw's sets of comparisons "is more obviously absurd than the first, and therefore carries the first down to its level of plausibility. Actually the comparisons sink both terms to equality at zero."[27] Ohmann notes the frequency of occurrence of this device and points out that in using it, Shaw "makes comparison count as both rhetoric *and* argument, by enclosing within it a miniature *reductio ad absurdum*" (235). Qian's final set of terms, then, by their rhetorical excess threaten to reduce all terms to insignificance. If lies are equal to rumors are equal to creativity are equal to morality, then the validity of the whole tissue of the essay is threatened. If morality and creativity are not really different—which has been the apparent main point of the essay up to now—then the certainty of all received values comes into question. The irony implicit in this method of discourse intends to raise just such doubts.

In constructing this argument, Qian has exaggerated the tradition of Chinese rhetoric with its predisposition to show parallels between disparate qualities. He has pushed the drawing of analogy to its logical end, where all distinctions cease to exist. This in turn brings up the logical paradox that if there are absolutely no distinctions, then the whole concept of similarity becomes meaningless. The purely rhetorical features of this paragraph, then, reveal themselves as being capable of proving or disproving anything, thereby casting the gravest doubts on the traditional contract between writer and reader. Thematically, however, this paragraph has a clear thrust. Since it was generally assumed in Chinese cosmogony that morality was superior to creativity—that the latter was, for that matter, but the vehicle of the former—the process of reducing them to equality—or even more pointedly, demonstrating that morality is but the vehicle of creativity—has a radical utility in undermining the traditional force of morality and all its specific manifestations. Qian's ultimate purpose of demolishing traditional stereotypes, creating more critical awareness and more careful readers, is thus well served by the ironic contrast between what he says and the implicit moral background.

The fifth paragraph begins by embellishing the ironic equilibrations of the qualities set forth in the fourth paragraph. With hypocrisy, morality, art and instruction all shaken from their normal contexts, Qian moves on to earnestly establish "true morality" and the pride which underlies it as the root of all human evil. He finishes the paragraph by affirming that hypocrites are superior to the "truly moral" in that they recognize their faults and can thus eventually reform themselves. But since he has already demolished "morality," when Qian goes on to say that "Moral hypocrisy can, therefore, be said to be the apprenticeship of true morality," we are left with another equation in which neither term can have any meaning.

Paragraph six:

[1] Therefore, those who are not fit to give moral instruction are the most suited to do so; the greater the hypocrite, the greater should be his attack on hypocrisy. [2] The defining characteristic of hypocrisy can be said to be shamelessness combined with a determination to have a sense of shame. [3] According to Shakespeare's Prince Hamlet's imprecation against his fiancee, women in making up want "face" while not being afraid to lose it [i.e., their natural one]: "God has given you one face, but you make yourself another." [4] Because of this, moral hypocrisy can be considered an art, along with cosmetology. [5] Like all art, however, this one has varying degrees of skillfulness; as the preface to the Roman poet Martial's collection of poetry says, "There is the extraordinarily good, there is the extraordinarily bad and there is the extraordinarily commonplace."

This final paragraph is in a diminished key; a final paradox in the first sentence, which is itself a weak extension to the more powerfully developed oppositions of the preceding paragraphs, keeps the sense of irony alive. The last sentence, which seems at first a non sequitur, upon reflection takes on a force which radiates back upon our experience of the essay as a whole: it is a final effort, necessarily unsuccessful, to reconcile the strong feelings brought out in the course of reading. The phrase "extraordinarily commonplace" mediates the Manichean atmosphere that pervades the essay's dealing in absolutes: its statement of ultimate relativism both recapitulates the affirmation-negation rhetoric of the essay and contrasts with the clearly implied theme. The phrase, in fact, underlines the central and unspoken paradox of this piece: Qian has just delivered himself of an impassioned moral teaching under the guise of attacking moral teaching; rhetoric and deeper theme have been at odds. While by their very nature (as well as by intention) these two cannot achieve any final harmony, this last and lyrical attempt to paper them over casts a retrospective light on them which confirms the reader's suspicion that there is nothing to be done about it, that all things are equal in their immunity to rational disposal. The endings of all of Qian's creative works have this characteristic ambiguity, a balancing which leaves the reader with a final sense of uncertainty, if only a sense of a void.[28]

As a whole, then, the essays display a resolution not to let down their irony. And in spite of the apparent randomness of the topics that come up for discussion, there is in them a consistent determination to expose the lazy conventional wisdom encompassed by traditional Chinese rhetoric and its continuing legacy in modern China. Qian carries this through by using many devices characteristic of the classical style to show how they distort reality. For all his parody of old forms, however, the care he takes to transmute elements of those forms into his vernacular style evinces a determination to transmit traditional richness of overtone to modern Chinese. The conscious refinement of Qian's literary language in *Tan Yi Lu* provides a vivid contrast to the experimental form of the "marginalia" and adds to the conviction that Qian directs part of his concern in the latter work to filling a poor vernacular with the supple expressiveness of the classical style. There is, in other words, a complex dialectic at work in these essays which attempts to keep alive the literary language's complexity of tone at the same time as mocking its obvious excesses.

To maintain these dual purposes, Qian concentrates on overcoming the side of classical prose that is all didactic formality. The essays, then, are meant to demonstrate conclusively that their "familiar" style belongs to belles lettres, where there is a creative gap between surface utterance and reader response. Qian's *Philobiblon* article, "The Return of the Native," offers direct proof that he did not wish informal prose to be taken at face value. After writing how metaphor may "undo" the philosopher, he goes on to say that

Austere writers on the art (ought we to say "science"?) of thought have been very emphatic on the danger of picture-thinking and the abuse of metaphor and analogy in reasoning. By a sleight of mental hand, thinkers often turn the juxtaposition of two things or situations into the substitution of one for the other. . . . In philosophy, . . . *comparaison n'est pas raison,* and inference by metaphor is of very doubtful validity.[29]

Final, philosophical conclusions, then, lie outside the scope of Qian's essays; but these writings *are* the means by which mental stagnation and circular thinking are to be exposed and thereby cleared away. Perhaps their most important message lies in Qian's steady avoidance of the portentous: even at his most serious he does not want his words fashioned into maxims. He could not be plainer about this than when he says in "Return": "It requires the most alert intelligence to keep a tentatively accepted hypothesis from turning into a firmly cherished dogma. This passion for finality and cocksureness is responsible for all philosophical fallacies and most political crimes" (22).

The situation confronting Qian was similar to that faced by Montaigne, Bacon and other post-Renaissance European prose reformers. Wishing to clear the literary stage of the twin problems of an intricate and self-referential classical language and an immature vernacular, this first generation to develop a complex vernacular was obliged to write a prose even more intricate and self-conscious than the literary language that had preceded it. Lu Xun, Qian, and others such as Fei Ming, Tang Tao and Wang Li sought to perform a similar task for modern China: they realized that real prose reform could not be achieved without meeting the peculiarities of the traditional language on its own ground.

Of these men, Qian in his "marginalia" goes farthest in the realm of being aware of and determined both to use and to push on traditional form itself. While the essays do not lack for underlying themes, their element of almost cold formal experimentation is something that the more passionate Lu Xun, for example, would never have been detached enough to indulge in. This experimentation eventually resulted, however, in the supple and controlled vernacular style which was to enable the extraordinary variety and power of expression in *Fortress Besieged*.

Chapter Five
The Stories

If post–May Fourth expository prose tended to mimic classical forms unconsciously, modern narrative has been marked by the opposite problem of a pronounced thinness of texture. There is a variety of reasons for this. Traditional literary prose, for one thing, was something which all educated men had to master and was therefore deeply ingrained; fiction writing, on the other hand, was a craft officially despised by the orthodoxy. Moreover, narrative involves depiction of people and events whose traditional models had been rendered obsolete by rapid social change. The different requirements of narrative as opposed to expository prose become clear in cataloguing the formal features of Qian Zhongshu's essays; it is difficult to imagine a style that undermines its own affirmations, contradicts itself, sets up paradoxes at will and is short and segmented being able to meet the demands of fiction for carefully delineated character, articulated narrative line and consistent tone. The problems with his short stories confirm that it was not an easy transition for him to make.

Satan, God, and Hades

The first piece in *Margin*, "Satan Pays an Evening Visit to Mr. Qian Zhongshu," meets the minimum requirements of representation in having a storyteller and a story. It consists of an extended dialogue between Qian and the devil in which Satan serially demolishes points of conventional wisdom as "Qian" brings them up. The author cannot resist the temptation to indulge his own pedantry by constructing the devil's character from satanic references in European literature that are duly cited. "Satan" differs from the other "marginalia" essays only in that the opinions expressed are put in quotation marks and made the substance of a dialogue between the narrator and the devil. This is a key structural difference, however. In the dialogue form, the bewildered figure of the narrator is allowed to take the part of straight-man that the reader must assume for himself in the essays. The figure of Qian speaks for the reader in expressing amazement at the outrageous assertions of the devil. For instance, when Satan complains that various authors through the ages have exposed so many of his personal secrets that "in the future, if I come to write an autobiography, I shall have to fabricate some astounding new facts," Qian in turn asks innocently whether such a process does not defy the meaning of the word "autobiography," to which Satan replies, "I did not expect your opinions to be so ordinary that they could fill newspaper editorials,"[1] and he goes on to explain how biography-writing has become debased. This is a common theme in Qian's writings and is clearly related to his basic concern with the dangers of deficiency in self-knowledge.

The dialogue form also allows for greater unity of development. The devil's initial statement about fabricating new facts is a *chedan,* announcing a transition to another topic. But instead of merely taking up the next topic—of the nature of biography—without any real introduction, Qian's query provides a natural bridge into the new discussion. In place of strictly pivoting on the final words of a previous utterance, the narrator's call for clarification sets up a narrative context; he does not leave the impression that the transition is simply the substitution of one related idea or word for another.

Perhaps the most prominent factor in making Qian's dialogue sequences seem to pursue a more natural course of development is their fidelity to typical speech patterns. With the exception of the satirical story "Linggan" [Inspiration], all of Qian's conversations adhere to the general rules of speech, in that each utterance does not carry on past the normal attention span an interlocutor in a conversation would be expected to observe.[2] Nor do they contain the elaborate images, punning and runaway progress that characterize Qian's essays. By confining itself almost exclusively to dialogue, "Satan" manages to finesse the problems involved with setting up a context for the representational development, which Qian's early creative work is rather short on; the careful reproduction of speech in this story manages to mask this lack more effectively than the dazzling display of rhetorical devices of some of the other stories.³ "Satan" is also for this reason a more amusing exposition of his themes than are his essays, but they pay a price for this appeal, forfeiting the ongoing alienation effect created by the unity of form and theme in the essays. The first-person narrator present in the tale serves as a lightning rod that dissipates some of the reader unease brought about by the powerful rhetoric of the essays.

If "Satan" establishes Qian's ability to construct dialogue successfully, the more serious representational questions such as story, plot and point of view are only confronted in the four stories collected in *Humans, Beasts and Ghosts*. Qian's thematic concerns in these stories, however, by and large overwhelm the attempt to create a mixed narrative basing itself upon rounded depiction of character interaction. The first story, "Shangdi de Meng" (God's Dream), is a lengthy exposition of the theme Satan enunciated in the tale discussed above when he lamented the reason that business had been so bad over the past hundred years: "By the mid-nineteenth century, there was suddenly a great change. Aside from a small minority, mankind almost completely lost its soul."⁴ The theme, in other words, adumbrates Qian's pessimistic sense that modern men have lost whatever values they may once have had. At the beginning of "God's Dream," he satirizes the resulting automatism by mocking the popular notion of evolution:

By that time, our world had been trained into submissiveness by the scientists, the philosophers and the political scientists; by the rules of the theory of evolution, the theory of creative evolution, the theory of organic evolution, eugenics and the New Life Movement, it [i.e., the world] had moved forward day by day. Today's way of life had superseded yesterday's; by afternoon the cultural standard of the morning had been raised.⁵

The Stories

The discussion moves on, in exactly the same "curt" style as do the essays, full of word play and pivot-words; the development lacks any real sense of narrative contexture.

It is not until the second page that Qian begins the representation of the story's main character, and even here he does so in the negative manner characteristic of the rhetorical undermining of the essays:

> The set rule of evolution is that the thing that comes later is superior. Out of time and space evolved inorganic matter; inorganic matter progressed to animals and plants; from fixed plants came quiet and clinging woman; from active animals came crude, adventurous man; man and woman creatively produced children; and dolls evolved from children. The supreme God, therefore, should be the last product of evolution. (2)

Here he abruptly bends the chain of evolving things that he had built up quite logically by switching the metaphor to the evolution of children and breaking it into absurdity when he reaches dolls. He couches the first mention of the existence of God in a cloud of ambiguity which leaves the reader confused as to whether God is indeed "supreme" or merely an entity subsisting somewhere in the deepest reaches of irony. Were this a text attempting to disprove the existence of God or a discursive satire of conventional theological ideas, the tone would be appropriate; but as the introduction to the principal actor in a story, it is too negative a series of propositions on which to build a functioning character.

One theme, however, comes through quite clearly: Qian shows rather bitterly that the mysticism whose absence he so laments in Chinese literature cannot be conjured up in an overly rational and unfeeling modern world. He exhibits a high sense of irony in setting forth all the devices of mysticism—God, the heavens, creation—only to undercut any possible substance to them. There is a further irony in his trotting out the full panoply of Western metaphysics only to negate it with the Buddhistic turn of showing everything to be illusory. For all the intellectual sophistication of this opening, however, Qian would have done well to remember his injunction in *Tan Yi Lu* to avoid direct "reasoned exposition" *(daoli)* in favor of a more subtle "sense of ideas" *(liqu)* generated through well-constructed imagery.

The representation of a world devoid of everything but this one, ultimate creature continues. As He achieves consciousness,

a habit left over from already extinct humankind instinctively awakened in God, and, like a baby, He cried out in fear [of the void that confronted Him]. But this silence, long unbroken by human sound, had congealed and allowed no noise to move in it. God realized that the external silence and His internal terror were both incubated by the darkness. And from this point on He hated the darkness and wished for the brightness which He had neither seen nor knew the name of. This wish grew stronger by the minute, and after a long period of time, the darkness weakened a bit, the night decreased its power, stealthily revealing the physiognomy of mountains and valleys; His eyes became functional and His field of vision produced something. God was surprised by this revelation of the greatness of His powers; He thought: He did not want darkness, and darkness discreetly gave way. . . . (3)

Here is the ambiguity once more: is God creator, or has He, Ah Q–like, taken credit for a natural process in which He took no part? This inconsistency results in a fictional world which leaves the reader uncertain as to how causality runs. This, of course, was the point of the essays, but to represent this theme successfully through the medium of plot and characters, Qian must at least first construct a sense of fictional world before he can demolish it. Similarly, character must be allowed to develop enough density to function consistently. The God in this story, however, at first seemingly representing an impotent solipsism, goes on actually to create a man and a woman (although Qian transparently attempts to finesse this inconsistency by having the creation take place only in God's dream), powers that the first few pages cause us to doubt conspicuously He could ever have.

God's dream creation of man and woman results from His vanity and consideration for His own loneliness: He wants someone to understand Him, praise him and be loyal to him, all at once. Thinking upon the problems involved in this, He falls asleep and creates man, whose first words are effulgent praise of his creator. But

> God did not realize that He was having a dream, or that the dream was having at Him. He did not know that, upon analysis, this ball of earth and water [i.e., man] was in the end nothing but the stuff of dreams. He had a dream of making man much as other people have dreams by accidentally tweaking their noses [while asleep]. God thought that He really had a person to cater to His every whim, that from now on praise did not have to issue from His own lips but would still be what He desired. Because the best praise of oneself seems to be what one wishes to say oneself, but, perversely, it must be heard from another; it must be as sincere and thorough as self-praise but contributed by someone else. We all have this ideal and we perhaps have all created people in our dreams to fulfill it; unfortunately we find it is not so easy to make this kind of person from nothing upon awakening. All we can do is take pre-existing people and reform them, or, at most, transform the little people who cater to us into great figures; neither of these courses is as satisfactory as dreaming. (6)

Structurally this paragraph is an example of digression on a pivot word. Beginning with the notion of God dreaming, the narrator takes off on a tangent by discussing the various facets of such dreams, leaving his story quite behind as he reaches out of it in direct appeal to the reader. The various faults adduced by fiction critics—telling as opposed to showing, direct authorial voice above the story and inconsistency of character development—are all present in this sample.

The theme of ideals as idle dreams that are at bottom nothing but vanity, however, does come through here. The ideals to which a powerfully conceived mystical realm can give substance are shown to be as devoid of substance as the metaphysical entities that are supposed to guarantee them. But the narrator here, rather than trying to wedge the causes and consequences of such behavior into some narrative context, too baldly pursues his themes. While the sense is clear and telling, such digressions from the narrative contribute to the development of neither God nor man, beings who must in the end carry the tale. Qian gives us one too many "corners" to evoke the full austerity of his vision.

The rest of the story continues in much the same manner. With the creation of man and woman come ever more possibilities for the narrator to set up anecdotes illustrating his themes: of the omnipresence of solipsism, of an entropy ensuring the failure of any act to achieve its intended result, of the total breakdown of any sensible causality and of the fundamental, negative equality of all things. Once man and woman have been created, however, there is dialogue among the three characters, which contrasts sharply, perhaps overly so, with the rich prose surrounding it. A good example of this is the first conversation between woman and God. It takes place after God has grown angry over the couple's increased blaséness toward the boons which He showers upon them without question. He has thus determined himself to refuse one of their requests and is eagerly anticipating the chance to disappoint them:

One day woman came alone to pay her respects to God. She sat at His feet, looking up at His face, liquid blue eyes like two drops of the Mediterranean, and said coquettishly:
"Lord, you are so good-hearted and your abilities are staggering; I really don't know how to thank you!"
God used His full strength to resist the onslaught of her flashing eyes and asked suspiciously, "What is it that you want?"
Woman, with apparent care, laughed ingratiatingly. It was a laugh which extended through her whole torso, adding a quiver to the full curves of her body. What she said seemed to float up on that laugh from the bottom of her heart, each word rising and falling with the laugh: "You really are the omniscient creator of all things! Nothing can be hidden from you, I really am awestruck. Actually there isn't anything that I really want. You've been good to us and we're completely satisfied—it really can't be considered a request." (10–11)

The description which prefaces the first utterance by woman is a bit overblown, but not seriously so. The lengthy interlude preceding her second speech, however, is not only so elaborate as to detract from the progress of the dialogue, it also adds nothing to what we already know: the insincerity of her flattery is quite apparent in the speech itself. This is especially the case in light of the fact that we have just been told that God is angry because of man's and woman's disregard of Him. It is as if Qian does not trust the reader to be able to sense the irony surrounding her remarks and that he feels himself obliged to draw our attention to it, reducing its force. This failure to achieve harmony in mixed narrative crops up repeatedly in Qian's fiction; it is perhaps the inevitable concomitant of a dual commitment to mimetic dialogue and a heavily ironic, critical backgrounding. When the mix is successful, as in many parts of *Fortress Besieged,* the dialogue floats on a high tide of irony set up by the obvious contrast between the background and what is being said. But too often Qian allows the background to obtrude in situations where plain dialogue would deliver the point more effectively. The authorial heavy-handedness resulting from this imbalance between representation and theme contrasts abruptly with Qian's care in *Tan Yi Lu* and in the "marginalia" collection to avoid forcing his opinions on the reader; the intrusiveness is another mark of his problems in adapting to the writing of fiction.

"God's Dream" ultimately falls victim to this inability to mediate representation, dialogue and theme successfully; theme dominates at the expense of the other two elements, and the tale cannot maintain its integrity either as fable or as story. In spite of these grave defects, however, the thematic material and the images through which it is expressed are so powerful that this story is perhaps the most piercing of all Qian's pre-*Fortress* work. Although the narrator is frequently unwilling to leave well enough alone, the story leaves a rich "sense of ideas."

Some of the most effective imagery appears in the prose frame which, at the beginning, sets the scene for the type of world of which God is coming into possession and, in the end, restates the same mood.[6] The ending, characteristically, carries the theme toward infinity—a type of ending common to all of Qian's fiction, as well as his essays. The scene setting opens with: "It was deep night. Ancient darkness securely covered the weak old world, like heavy eyelids hanging on eyes in need of sleep" (2). The finale returns to this tonic key, includes God within its scope and leads us beyond it into eternity: "God stretched himself awake and heaved a long, weary yawn at this dead, sinking sun and world long devoid of life. He opened His mouth wide, as if to devour in a gulp the limitless and hard-passing time" (20). The short lives of the man and woman rounded by this sleep clamor futilely against cosmic indifference; it is the space between noise and silence which moves us. Within this contrast, even the loquacity of the narrator adds to the overwhelming chorus of human inadequacy.

The third story in the collection, "Inspiration," also employs an otherworldly scene—in this case Hell—in which to develop its satire of the contemporary literary culture. C. T. Hsia points out the tale's thematic similarity with Dryden's *Mac Flecknoe,* Pope's *The Dunciad* and Byron's *The Vision of Judgement,*[7] but the differences between Qian's creation and those of the English poets are as instructive as the similarities. The European satires of contemporary taste are full of allusions to classic works and the resonant images of Western culture, while Qian gives his sense of humor free rein and draws a series of ad hoc images largely through elaborate word play. The result is marked by the same lack of overtone that Qian is criticizing, for although satire means to create a negative image and does not therefore require the same extensive character and plot development as does positive representation,[8] "Inspiration" is deficient even by the reduced standards of its genre.

A typical instance of development by and for the sake of word play comes in a passage where the protagonist—a recently dead hack, but very popular writer—asks the King of Hell why he sports a long black beard. The king replies:

You must know that the symbol of the Western judiciary is a white wig worn on the head. You must also know of those famous works that discourse on Chinese culture for the sake of foreigners. Does one not understand from them that our nation, people, customs and psychology are all the opposite of the West? We are an oriental people, they insist on being occidental; we are of the Middle Kingdom, they persist in being outsiders; when we wave, our hands point downward, when they wave they stubbornly point their hands upward; when we pay obeisance we bend our legs, when they salute, on the other hand, they raise their arms; when their bachelors propose marriage, they get down on their knees, our men are punished by their wives after marriage by being forced to kneel; as you can see, absolutely everything is topsy-turvy. . . . When we die mourners wear white, when they die mourners wear black; therefore, if their impartial judges wear wigs on their heads, our upholders of justice such as myself should grow natural black beards under their chins. Doing this, we will not have to apologize to those who compare Eastern and Western cultures for bringing about the destruction of the rule that they have induced. (102)

While this series takes aim at the dealers in easy cultural generalities that comprise one of Qian's favorite targets, it removes itself too far from the principal focus of the satire—the stylistic poverty of modern Chinese authors. The blatant parody of parallel structure in this passage recalls the self-conscious undermining of the essays, but its forced use in the context of representation tends to get in the way; since "Inspiration" is a story, the manipulation of a simple image through all its possible permutations results in a humor often too facile for its own good.

"Souvenir"

The other two stories in the collection, "Mao" [The Cat] and "Jinian" [Souvenir], however, both move resolutely into the realm of representation; they present consistent and well worked-out plots. In them, Qian achieves more control over the various elements of fiction writing and makes real progress toward the harmonization of narrative devices that is to reach fruition in *Fortress Besieged*.

The plot of "Souvenir," the fourth piece in the collection, is basically an extended flashback of the events leading up to the forcible consummation of an affair involving the heroine and her husband's air force pilot cousin, Tianjian. The final pages of the story end it with the irony of the discovery by the woman, Manqian, that she is pregnant by Tianjian, soon after learning that he has been shot down and killed. Manqian's good-hearted and innocent husband Caishu suggests naming the child Tianjian, should it be a boy. Manqian refuses by citing Tianjian's questionable activities with a local air force camp follower.

The tale opens with Manqian returning home and ruefully going over in her mind the sequence of events which caused the situation to get out of her control and end in a denouement most distasteful to her. Of the story's thirty-seven pages, fully twenty-eight of them consist of retrospective narrative; this whole long sequence is, in effect, enclosed in a frame which casts over all the events contained within it the mood of passive chagrin characterizing Manqian. This framing technique was also used in "God's Dream," but it is only in "Souvenir" that Qian turns it to full representational effect. The first paragraph establishes the scene:

Although it was a city surrounded by layer upon layer of tall mountains, in the spring it seemed as though enemy planes were able to make their attacks unobstructed and, what's more, even earlier than in other places. It is sad to relate that these arid mountains were not suited to cultivation; thus, when spring came, there was no place to hide. Closely following upon a dreary and steamy Lantern Festival [held fifteen days after the lunar new year], then, came these few days of fine sunlight, which gradually brought a sense of spring to the mountain town. In the continuing clear days, the busy dust particles suspended in the air of the surrounding mountains were illuminated by the rays of the evening sun, imparting to the atmosphere a deep yellow haze, mellow as wine. It was a fine time, when one could dream while awake and be drunk without the use of alcohol. (120)

The filiation with the ironic openings of Qian's other prose pieces is clear here; beginning with a statement of the treachery of spring, the time of enemy bombings, he moves beyond this to describe the true delights of the season. It is a characteristic juxtaposition of unexpected consequences: the glorious weather brings terror.

This descripton of the languors of spring, however, has another function. It leads into the introduction of Manqian and serves as a naturalistic correlative to her character. The second paragraph brings her on the scene:

Manqian turned into the small alley from the large street on which the sun lingered. The presence of the sun had long since dissipated from the alley and the spring chill of early evening surprised her. It was only then that she realized that she had somehow or other reached her residence. She did not know how she had come; her legs were very sore. The uneven cobblestone had hurt her feet while at the same time causing her some anxiety. This was because she was wearing the high-heeled shoes that she had purchased the year before last while passing through Hong Kong; they were her last luxury before coming into the interior. (120)

"Dreaming while awake" thus serves as a pivot from the weather to Manqian's character.

After having once moved from the ominousness of the prospect of the bombing to the beauty of the weather, the description shifts here once more—once the sun sets, chill returns and the mood darkens again. The added note about the concern for her shoes, analogous to the digressions found in Qian's earlier writings, serves an important function in this situation by rounding out the depiction of her character. Whereas such digressions set the plot off-track in Qian's satirical stories, here they contribute to psychological naturalism through being lodged in the thoughts of a character. The desultory pettiness of the thought matches the desultory pettiness of mind that Manqian will exhibit throughout the story.

The concluding segment of this narrative frame, while returning the scene to the present, echoes the themes set forth in the opening passages; by beginning and ending the flashback on the same note, Qian succeeds in imparting a mood of lassitude, random lack of foresight, and expectation gone awry:

Their love had been consummated, and, with that, was over. . . . Manqian . . . did not think of the future. She went home without stopping and collapsed on her bed. Her mind was as clear as if it had been washed with ice water and she knew that she didn't love Tianjian. Moreover, the vanity which had caused her to seek to win Tianjian's love had now vanished without a trace. The events that had just passed left a shadow on her emotions, as if imprinting on them a thin layer of Tianjian. She didn't know when this hateful feeling would recede. In a short time Caishu would return; she didn't know how she could face him. (151–52)

This passage parallels the earlier one. Love-making, presumably engaged in to bring on a feeling like the spring air, has instead, like the clearing of the air which has allowed the coming of enemy bombers, an effect totally at odds with expectation. Just as she walks from the sunlit street into the cold alley, the chill occurring after the act clears her mind. The second passage ends on a note as trivial and as typical as the first. Instead of any real guilt or consideration of consequence, Manqian is only concerned with how she will hide her feelings from her guileless husband; as she thought to herself slightly earlier, "lying straight to his face seemed much harder than cheating on him behind his back" (122).

In the flashback sequences which comprise the main body of the text, certain other narrative methods are employed which have their roots in the prose techniques of the essays. They gain a new resonance, however, from the careful development of context. In the following passage, which recounts Manqian's meditations upon returning home and seeing the mud wall which surrounds their house, Qian's technique of moving his prose forward by pivoting off word association achieves a new level:

In this place, where bricks were rare, mud walls were common. But in contrast with the brick and stone walls of their neighbors, this mud wall, so unconscious of its own wretchedness, had caused its mistress many embarrassing moments. When they were originally considering renting the place, Manqian thought the wall ugly. The landlord was sensible of her opposition and thereupon lowered the rent; it was due, then, to this wall that the house had been rented at all. By now, she had made her peace with the wall and accepted its protection. Her husband Caishu not only accepted the simple earth barrier, but became its advocate: he was proud of it, he boasted about it—in other words, he wasn't willing to accept it, but covered [his feelings] with his praise. (121)

This pivot, which begins with Manqian seeing the wall, is neither a diversion nor a simple mood-reinforcer: it contributes actively to the progress of the narrative by bringing Caishu into the story and telling us a few things about him. Equally importantly, it describes as well how the husband's and wife's respective characters differ: Manqian concerned with appearances and not easily contented, Caishu willing, too willing, to accept his lot. The paradox inserted in the narrative—that Caishu serves as the wall's advocate precisely because he is not finally happy with it—although a *chedan,* has more than just shock value directed toward upsetting the reader's sense of the norm. It also has the function, internal to the text, of giving us a key insight into his psychological makeup. The pivot word is thus elevated to a symbol.

It is also in this story that Qian first succeeds in combining his ear for dialogue with the sense of portraying the process of thinking going on before us which is so prominent a feature of the essays. The result is narrated monologue, a technique characterized by use of the third person and the past tense common to narration, but which simultaneously employs the "syntactical structure . . . of direct discourse, with the rhythms of spoken language rendered through exclamations, rhetorical questions, repetitions . . . and exaggerated emphases."[9] This mode, "by maintaining the person and tense of authorial narration, . . . enables the author to recount the character's silent thoughts without a break in the narrative thread" (98). Thus, "by allowing the same tense to describe the individual's view of reality and that reality itself, inner and outer world become one, eliminating explicit distance between the narrator and his creature" (99).

The first occurrence of this narrative form is near the beginning of the story, shortly after an account of the increasing shabbiness of Manqian's clothes:

The fur coat was about to lose its fur and the color of the velvet *qipao* was fading. The place had become more lively since last summer. Along with the retreating government officers came any number of stylish women and young ladies—enough to dazzle the eyes of the local folk. Manqian wore the clothes, both inside and out, that she had brought with her upon marriage, and she of course wished to add a few more fashionable garments. Her dowry, however, had long since been used in paying for their escape [from enemy-held territory], and Caishu's monthly wage was only enough to cover expenses. *How could there be any left over to make some clothes that would please her?* She was considerate of her husband, not only did she not make any demands of him, but she didn't even let him know. *Yes, in two years of marriage she hadn't lived many comfortable days.* But she patiently endured beside Caishu, used her pride to maintain her love and never complained to anyone. *This type of wife can't be said to have wronged her husband!* [Emphasis added.] (123–24)

Every sentence in this passage is written in a style more characteristic of Qian's dialogue than of his narrative exposition; there are no puns, no images or metaphors, no self-conscious digressions. The three sentences underlined, in particular, display all the hallmarks of narrated monologue, where changing person from third to first would make totally plausible monologue. In spite of such occasional and vivid entries into her mind, however, Qian never completely withdraws the irony of his descriptions of Manqian's musings, and the reader is thus unable to develop any real sympathy for the character.

As a result, for all of "Souvenir" 's technical success, as a whole it is less than fully satisfactory because of the narrator's excessive detachment. The flashback technique is not handled with sufficient lightness of touch: knowing the denouement from the beginning, we are not compensated for the lack of suspense by full enough depiction of the heroine's inner struggles. Her passivity, alluded to again and again and reinforced structurally by the static and exterior descriptions of her mental state, at last renders her almost inert to the reader; it becomes difficult to maintain interest. The several ironic episodes, such as Manqian's initial lack of interest in meeting Tianjian, eventually seem too *deus ex machina*. Since none of the characters is brought fully to life, such irony draws inordinate attention to itself as it marches the plot forward. While the entropy, the failure of expectation and rational consequence, the pettiness of human activity and the self-delusion that characterized life in Republican China are all clearly expressed by the continually recurring irony and personal defeat that the story relates, the characters who are their victims are not vivid enough to bring these themes fully to life. In the end, even the dour mood frame that surrounds the events is so heavy that it crushes the life out of the events themselves.

"The Cat"

The second story in the collection, "The Cat," although full of technical flaws, is the most interesting of the lot. It moves firmly out onto the ground that *Fortress* will cover so successfully because it manages both to throw light on Qian's constant themes and to view them in the focus of contemporary events. Whereas the other prose pieces had treated these problems as eternal to the Chinese nation, if not to the world, the dominant tension and irony in "The Cat" is provided by the contrast between the lives and thoughts of the story's characters and the onrushing course of events in the spring of 1937, the few months before the beginning of the war.

The stuff of the story, like that of "Souvenir," is rather simple: Li Aimo and her husband Li Jianhou keep a salon in Peiping, where the various eminences of the "Capital Clique" (*Jing Pai*) foregather to tend the fires of modern Chinese culture.[10] Jianhou, long in his wife's shadow, decides to write his memoirs in order to make a name for himself and hires a young secretary, Yigu, to assist. Aimo takes a fancy to the young man and increasingly usurps his time. Jianhou, realizing that he lacks the ability to complete the book on his own, eventually flares up at his wife. They have a fight and he soon thereafter departs for the south with a young girl friend he had recently acquired. Aimo is told the news when the worshipful Yigu is in attendance, and she seeks psychological revenge by taking the young man as lover. In spite of this having been the subject of his fantasies over the preceding weeks, Yigu has a sudden realization of the tawdriness of the situation and backs out just when his desires are capable of being fulfilled.

Only thirty-three of the tale's sixty-eight pages, however, are devoted to the development of this plot. This thirty-three-page unit taken alone would constitute a story similar in length and composition to "Souvenir." Inserted in its midst, however, is what is in effect a thirty-five-page digression depicting a tea party with various members of the "Capital Clique" in attendance. It is a static scene; the first fifteen pages consist of capsule descriptions of each character as he enters the room and the remainder of clever banter. But the puffery and inconsequence of the talk take on thick dramatic irony when we realize that it all takes place in the shadow of a catastrophic war that is to wipe these people out as a class. The effect is heightened by the fact that these characters are transparent caricatures of actual people in the contemporary Peiping intellectual establishment. The power evoked by this representation of collision between time and temperament gives the story its strength.

As in "Souvenir," the story's first fourteen pages are a flashback, which allows the construction of a mood frame through a pregnant and symbol-filled opening. The story takes on substance as the narrative progresses and contextual detail fills in. "The Cat" begins with Yigu examining tattered remnants of the manuscript of Jianhou's "book," which the younger man has just finished drawing up, only to have Aimo's precious cat "Darkie" tear it into shreds. The cat's symbolic association with Aimo and Aimo's carelessly destructive attitude toward her husband are clearly established in the first paragraph. The narrative goes on to relate the background of Aimo and Jianhou's marriage and the process by which Yigu has been hired, in a flippant style that becomes overly clever in the manner of "Inspiration." It goes on to recount Yigu's eventual loss of respect for Jianhou and his invitation to the tea party which forms the tale's centerpiece. With the issuance of the invitation, the narration shifts into a brief narrated monologue which deals with Yigu's fears at being in the presence of such august personages. This sequence serves to fix the consciousness center of the narration in Yigu, and it is through his impressionable eyes that we see and hear the party.

Perception does not center completely in Yigu's mind, however; the narrator is unwilling to forfeit completely his own omniscience and authority to pass judgment at will. For instance, after he has depicted the characters of Aimo and Jianhou in the most scathing and supercilious terms, the narrator sums up Yigu's transformed opinion of Jianhou as follows:

These two-and-a-half days of work totally wiped out the respectful attitude that Yigu had harbored toward Jianhou. The rashness of youth caused him to despise mercilessly his employer; he could see Jianhou's vapidness, his vanity, his lack of intelligence, while overlooking Jianhou's good points as a man and in the way he treated people. He should have been grateful for Jianhou's willingness to hire him at quite a good wage to perform this quite inessential task. But he only resented Jianhou's possession of money and the power it gave him to sacrifice the mental energy of youth to help him write this useless stuff. (35)

There are two problems with this passage. The first is the obtrusiveness of the narrator: Yigu's priggish ingratitude to Jianhou's gracious treatment is obvious from the context and does not require explicit underlining. The second is that, prior to this, we have been led by the narrator to have precisely the same view of Jianhou as Yigu takes here; Qian is at some pains to signal to us at every turn that Jianhou is a fatuous bumbler. Put together, the result is a gratuitous dig at Yigu, who up to this point has been for us a "reliable commentator."[11] What almost seems to be Qian's inability to trust his reader to draw the right conclusions throws awry the delicate balance between the interior world of the protagonist and the exterior world of the narrator.

Shortly after Yigu's interior monologue, the party begins. As each member of the crew shows up, the narrator draws a portrait of him which is in most cases so unambiguous that even a reader forty years removed from the scene can name the person or combination of persons being lampooned. This is in spite of Qian's disingenuous and highly ironic preface to the collection, in which he counsels readers against trying to draw parallels between the book's characters and real people.[12] Compare, for instance, Kai-yu Hsu's recent description of Shen Congwen with "Cat" 's Cao Shichang. As Hsu recalls Shen in 1940: "The famous thirty-eight-year-old writer, a tiny, thin man wearing metal-rimmed glasses, spoke so softly that even we in the first row had to lean forward and strain to hear him."[13] Qian's description of Cao is as follows:

The lovely and seductive voice of the dainty Cao Shichang was enough to delude a man's heart if heard through a wall. But actually seeing a male talk in such a delicate voice caused impatience in many who wished that, as with a radio, they could reach over and turn up his sound. (44)

Other participants include thinly disguised versions of Zhou Zuoren, Lin Yutang, and the political writer Luo Longji.

The conversation that ensues is a skillful combination of mimetic dialogue and the undermining technique that characterized the essays, in this respect rather like "Satan." The number and variety of participants, however, as well as the topicality of the discussion, make it much more successful than the earlier piece. A scheme is set up in which the guests argue with and refute one another, rendering each point made suspect and thus incapable of being accepted by the audience; furthermore, the contrast between the talk and the eventual course of events provides an irony to the whole scene. For instance, in the episode's first serious discussion, forthcoming only after the guests have taken various potshots at the political commentator—their general thrust being that they doubt his credibility—he agrees at last to give his opinions on the political situation as of spring 1937. He begins by saying, "I don't think that war will break out immediately" (54) and goes on to give his four reasons for so thinking: first, the Chinese are not yet fully prepared; second, the Soviet Union would take action in the event of a Japanese invasion; third, the United States and the United Kingdom would not sit by passively, but would assist China actively; and fourth, the Chinese government is on good terms with Hitler and Mussolini, Japan's allies, so those European powers would not interfere with American and British assistance to China. He sums up by saying that "I do not expect from what I can observe that war will break out within the next two or three years. But of course, there are always things which happen that escape our calculation"(55).

The last sentence is a *chedan* serving to vitiate the certainty of the apparently positive statements that had preceded it. The other characters react to it accordingly. Having listened to Ma Yongzhong (the commentator) with increasing confidence, they express frustration at having this confidence undermined. Thus the *chedan*, which was a matter between the author and reader exclusively in the essays, is made a vital aspect of the representation here because it is part of the interaction between characters. The power of the passage is increased by the contextual irony with which the 1946—or later—audience reads the exchange, knowing that all four of Ma's pieces of evidence were nothing more than the pious expression of political weakness which failed when they were needed.[14] The conversation continues along like this, with the exception that the rebuttals to each positive utterance come from another speaker rather than consisting of self-contradiction as in the case of Ma. The final impression left on the reader by this lengthy episode is reminiscent of Jean Renoir's classic film, *Rules of the Game:* it is a piece of historical pathos, with the players, sitting so confidently as if in full possession of their destinies, clearly perceived by the outsider as being trapped by the worst sort of self-delusion. Situating the story at this historical juncture gives it the full force of the "pregnant moment" that Qian was later to analyze in "Reading *Laocoon.*"

After the departure of the guests, the story returns to its original focus on the Lis' and Yigu. Soon Aimo is having the student perform so many tasks for her that he has no time to work on Jianhou's travel diary. This leads to a fight between the couple which is a masterpiece of representational economy and pointed dialogue. It occupies a key point in the plot in that it represents the final rupture of their relationship, through Jianhou's realization of his inferior position:

Jianhou sat up and said, "I hired the secretary, so I should be able to tell him what to do. If I don't allow him to do odd jobs for you, that's up to me."

Aimo put down her cigarette to free her mouth for the argument and said, "As long as you hired him at all, I'll use him if I have something for him to do. As a matter of fact, the things you're having him do are even more useless than the work I give him. If you have it in you to write a book, do it yourself and don't expect somebody else to do it for you."

Jianhou hit the bed in anger and said, "Okay, fine! I'll fire him tomorrow, no secretary for anybody."

Aimo said, "If you let him go, I'll hire him. I have a lot of things to be done. Compared with your travel diary—"

Jianhou said, "If you're so busy, why don't you hire your own secretary instead of imposing on mine?"

Aimo said, "My dear husband, if we can economize why not economize? I'm not the type of woman to just throw money away. And for that matter, I'm not aware of ever having separated my household from yours."

Jianhou said, "Since you bring it up, I do wish that the lines between us were drawn a bit more clearly."

Aimo stood up and said, "Jianhou, don't say anything you'll regret later."

Jianhou realized that he had spoken too harshly, but, refusing to concede, said, "Don't twist my words and make a mountain out of a molehill." (76–77)

At this point Aimo offers to give up using Yigu, but Jianhou says:

Don't counterfeit benevolence. I'm not going back to the study because I'm going out. If you want to use Yigu, use him all you want. I'm not going to write anything anymore. Everything would end up the same anyway—any fame I might achieve would be usurped by you. Just like our friends, they're all yours, they really don't have anything to do with me at all; even the servants all do what you tell them to first and put off anything I might tell them to do. It's a good thing we don't have any children because they'd all be like animals or savages, they'd only know they had a mother and wouldn't even recognize their old man. (78)

In the next few days after the fight, Jianhou spends most of his time out of the house, and it is soon thereafter that one of the members of the salon, Chen Xiajun, comes to tell Aimo that her husband has run off with a young girl. Aimo reaches out automatically to Yigu to gain her revenge and, in so doing, scares him off. With this, she suddenly feels her age and thinks only of seeking out a place where she can hide from life. This denouement richly sums up the particular ironies of the story. Yigu suddenly sees that he does not want what he thought he wanted even as it comes within reach; Aimo's desperate act ends up being more demeaning than she could have imagined. There is no dignity for these characters even in the loss of their illusions.

The story closes by portraying Jianhou the day after he leaves Peiping in a powerful scene encapsulating the entropy and futility which Qian sees as the essence of life. But the scene also has specific, temporal implications that capture a moment of historical revelation and sum up the universal side of the tale: the older generation, no wiser for what they know is coming, rush willy-nilly into it, led by youth, whose naive enthusiasm is only momentarily beguiling:

By that time, the train which had yesterday left Peiping had entered Shantung. Li Jianhou was looking out the window, his spirit as pinched and arid as the yellow dust which flew past. Yesterday's excitement, like the happiness of drink, left only chagrin when it was over. Thinking that Chen Xiajun would certainly tell Aimo, Jianhou realized that the whole business would get out of hand and he would have no way to recover himself. What a waste to break up a family for the sake of this plain and immature girl who sat beside him! He regretted his rashness— one moment of indulgence and things wound up this way. The girl, holding his hand while looking out the window, was wholly insensible of his thoughts. She could only consider how life's future, like the endless journey of the train, stretched boundlessly before her. (88)

This passage can almost make an aesthetic totality out of a story which is essentially a collection of diffuse units.

In sum, while Qian did not altogether master the craft of narrative in these stories, he was remarkably successful in bending some of the structural elements of his satirical essays to the purposes of fiction. He brought his mordant themes to the stories as well, although they are oftentimes too much with us. Only in his masterpiece, *Fortress Besieged,* however, do theme, narrative, and dialogue achieve satisfactory cohesion. It is to that work that we now turn.

Chapter Six
Fortress Besieged

The novel *Fortress Besieged*, which took Qian "fully two years" of his wartime sojourn in Shanghai to write,[1] succeeds in turning his various concerns as an author into what many today regard as modern China's greatest novel. Not only do his vernacular style and enduring themes reach fruition in this work, but it also makes the definitive comment on Qian's class in his time. He accomplishes this the more remarkably largely without explicit reference to the physical suffering or the great political struggles of the war. As he said of the book in 1979, he tried to have "the war at once remote and impinging, like the Napoleonic Wars in the novels of Jane Austen."[2] Qian in this way achieves the aesthetic "pregnancy" of leaving the reader to fill in the obvious. The novel creates a powerful impression of the frivolity of the Chinese urban middle class on the eve of the war and of its incapacity to deal with the war's demands—a group that matures in knowledge even as it loses its ability to cope with the reality it belatedly is coming to recognize. Qian himself, writing in 1940, gives explicit voice to the sense of time usurped before it could be well spent:

[Prewar] years so pleasant to recall, and yet so curiously remote: for the War, while most efficiently shortening human lives, gives one also a specious feeling of longevity, the feeling of having lived very long from being made to outlive a good deal in a short while. I only regret now with a wisdom after the event that I had done but niggardly justice to those years in not spending them to some better purpose.[3]

Fortress Besieged: The Story

A detailed account of *Fortress* must begin with a brief synopsis of the novel's plot. The book is divided into nine chapters, which combine roughly into five of what Roland Barthes calls "functional sequences."[4] There is a symmetry to this structure: the final two segments are negative images of the first two, with the third acting as a watershed.

The first sequence comprises the first three-and-a-half chapters and relates the rather scattered series of events which befall the protagonist Fang Hongjian (it is from Fang's viewpoint that the novel unfolds) during his return journey to and subsequent residence in Shanghai in 1937–38. Chapter 1 begins on the boat; it serves to introduce the ineffectual Fang and place him directly into a triangular relationship with two women returning on the same ship. One of them is the rather Europeanized and ostentatious Miss Bao, the other the more refined and hesitant Su Wenwan, a college classmate of Fang's who is coming home after having received a doctorate from a French university. Fang had gone to Europe on the dowry money which his would-be in-laws had decided to present to him in spite of his fiancée's death. In Europe for four years, he had spent time in England, France, and Germany without having engaged in any serious study. Only after he found his money running low and had decided to return to China did he realize the importance of a doctorate, both to his own parents and to his "in-laws." Just before returning, therefore, he had purchased a fraudulent degree, intending to use it strictly to deceive his family with and then to forget it.

Once on the ship, the more forward Miss Bao, in spite of the fact that she is engaged, manages to win out over Miss Su in the competition for Fang. Bao and Fang thereupon have a brief and secret affair which becomes unpleasant as soon as it is consummated. The chapter ends with the arrival of the ship at Hong Kong and Bao's reunion with her fiancé; Fang, who had not been able to reconcile himself to Bao's increasing coldness to him as they approached home, is provoked by his mixed emotions, in spite of himself, into asking Su Wenwan to accompany him for the day during the brief stopover in Hong Kong.

The second chapter portrays the return to Shanghai; it introduces us to Fang's family and to his "in-laws," the Zhous'. The contrasts between the scholarly Fangs'—Hongjian's father has the *juren* degree—and the newly rich, mercantile Zhous' are sharply drawn, as is the Fangs' contempt for the other family. The Zhous', for instance, had had the news of Hongjian's "degree" splashed prominently in the Shanghai newspapers, something that mortifies the young man with his highly developed sense of propriety.

This chapter is essentially composed of two picaresque episodes that result from Hongjian's lackadaisical behavior in situations which he cannot bring himself to take seriously. The first episode is a speech which he gives on the history of Western influence in China to his old high school.[5] Having misplaced his notes, all he can remember are a few outrageously incorrect opinions on the matter that he had culled the night before from a desultory reading of some late Qing scholarship. The second episode is occasioned by an attempt by Mrs. Zhou at matchmaking which sends Hongjian to dinner at the home of a Shanghai comprador for an American company; the family's aping of American ways and speech patterns is meticulously recorded. Both these episodes deal with the misplacement and misunderstanding of foreign values in China, a motif that the novel shares with contemporary intellectual opinion.

Neither character nor situation is taken very seriously in this chapter, however, the narrative tone is casually derisive, and Hongjian jumps from scene to scene without the vaguest thought about any consequences that his actions might have. This tone, in fact, characterizes the first sequence as a whole, in spite of the fact that the action takes place just as the most catastrophic war in modern Chinese history is beginning. The third chapter is continuous with the second. It opens, furthermore, on the same note as that on which the first chapter had ended: Hongjian, in spite of his fears of her designs upon him, seeking out Su Wenwan for lack of anything better to do. Upon his first visit to her house, however, another triangle is forthwith set up when he encounters her young cousin Tang Xiaofu and becomes instantaneously infatuated with her. The entrance on the scene of Zhao Xinmei, recently returned from America with a degree in political science and the son of a fellow-official of Su Wenwan's father, further complicates the relationship. The resulting situation absurdly has Zhao pursuing Su without success while the latter pursues Fang, who, in turn, only has eyes for Tang, a proud young woman who is not about to be won over easily. This set of relationships represents the most fundamental of the novel's leitmotifs: the constant human pursuit of what is unattainable and discontent with what is directly at hand.[6] The relationships also serve as a backdrop to a series of conversations held at various salons which caricature contemporary Shanghai intellectual circles in a manner similar to "The Cat."

The chapter concludes with a rapidly narrated series of events which close out all of Hongjian's options in Shanghai. Lacking the courage to tell Su of his true intentions (or lack thereof) toward her, Fang had allowed the situation to develop in such a way that when he finally tells her, her fury is such that she immediately proceeds to slander Hongjian to her cousin and thus cause that relationship also to terminate abruptly. Su almost as quickly accepts the proposal of another suitor, and Zhao's hopes are thereby similarly dashed. The fourth chapter continues the narration of these climactic events. Hongjian, who had been living in the Zhous' home and working at their bank, wishes to be alone with his hurt. Consequently he takes every possible measure to avoid the insatiably curious Mrs. Zhou; her resulting angry frustration precipitates a final split between the two families. Just before this series of fractures, however, Hongjian had, much to his surprise, received an appointment to a professorship at a newly opened national university in rural Hunan, and, as everything in Shanghai has foreclosed on him, he decides to accept it. It turns out that Zhao, hoping to remove what he thought to be his most serious competition for the hand of Su Wenwan, had submitted Hongjian's name to the school. Now that Zhao has lost out as well, he decides to go along to take a post of his own at the university.

The remainder of the short fourth chapter provides transition to the second sequence by winding up business in Shanghai and portraying the preparations for the trip. As part of the latter, the three characters who are to accompany Fang and Zhao to the interior are introduced. Two of them, Li Meiting and Gu Erqian, are academic impostors (Li, for instance, carries along with him the drawerful of file cards of which Qian had been so contemptuous in the essay "Discussing Friendship"), and the third, the only woman of the group, Sun Roujia, is a recent college graduate who is going to serve as a teaching assistant. The moral degeneracy of Li and Gu sets the tone for the second sequence, which consists of the narration of the journey and is completely contained in the fifth chapter. This segment is composed almost entirely of a series of picaresque episodes which humorously accentuate the enormous differences between the pre-war Chinese urbanized elite and the more traditional people of the interior. The narrative tone in this sequence, however, has more bite to it than that of the first: from the perspective of Fang Hongjian, whose sense of propriety is matched only by his self-contempt, associating with the likes of Li and Gu and the assorted rogues the group encounters even further lowers Fang's estimation of himself. The blithe disregard for consequence that marks the first sequence turns to an increasing introspection.

The mood of the third sequence, which occupies the fifth and sixth chapters and relates the events of the academic year at Sanlü University, brings together elements of both the first two segments. The satire of manners of the beginning chapters is combined with the corroding pettiness of the travel episodes to provide simultaneously the sharpest satire and the most dismal environment of the book. This section provides the transition from the predominantly humorous first half of the book to the pathos of the last part. It is events in this middle section which determine Fang's decline. Although Fang and Zhao behave as if they were still in Shanghai, the restricted dimensions of their environment no longer allow the same facile disregard of consequence. Every word uttered and every action taken are recorded and become part of their immediate fates. Because of their cavalier attitude, the two men continually run afoul of local mores; it is only a matter of time before the situation snaps back at them. This happens eventually when Zhao Xinmei is caught in a compromising position with the wife of the head of the Chinese department; he leaves in a huff. With the more powerful Zhao gone, Hongjian's enemies take advantage of his solitariness to arrange for the nonrenewal of his contract. In this sequence, as in the first, the climactic events are run off at the end at top narrative speed: the situations which had developed at such a dilatory pace and without apparent purpose come together suddenly and exact their price. In this process of closing, Hongjian is caught in a position with Roujia which is a pallid copy of Zhao's imbroglio, with the different result that Fang and Sun become engaged.

The fourth sequence is contained in the eighth chapter; it consists of the narration of Hongjian and Roujia's return journey, via Hong Kong again, to Shanghai. The happiness of the new couple together is quickly glossed over, and the story becomes a record of the sources of the marital discord which dominates the fifth sequence. Upon passing through Hong Kong they encounter Zhao Xinmei, who, fearing the possible fruits of the couple's cohabitation, urges immediate marriage upon Hongjian. Fang and Su do eventually marry in Hong Kong, but the difficulties of managing the whole business alone in a strange place put such a strain on the relationship as to sour it permanently. They also run into Su Wenwan, and it is at this meeting that a horrible truth emerges that has hitherto been mostly obscured by the story's horizontal progress: we now see, through the eyes of Hongjian and Roujia, Su Wenwan as a great and rich lady who towers above the newlyweds in social state. Fang's continual running from the consequences of his actions has now come full circle, and we can view through his own eyes the extent to which his incessant movement has been a downward spiral as well. And in the vicious class society whose gradations have been so carefully set forth, the realization is stunning. However, the corruption of the social level from which he has fallen (and, by extension, of the whole society) is made manifest at the same time: Su maintains her social position only by smuggling merchandise from Hong Kong to Chungking.

The sense of a cycle completed is reinforced by the scene on the boat from Hong Kong to Shanghai which marks the end of the eighth chapter. It has now been two years since Hongjian's return from Europe on a similar ship, and one year from the time that they commenced their journey to the interior, also by sea. Fang muses on the contrasts between the three occasions, and the reader cannot help filling in the details. The first return, in a frivolous mood, was accompanied by a sense of complete openness of opportunity. The departure, while chilled a good deal by the foreshortening of Hongjian's Shanghai horizons, was still marked at least by the residual optimism of being able to leave and try something new. But the second return is stifling; opportunities have dried up both in Shanghai and elsewhere, and he is confronted with the prospect of starting again against a background of complete failure. Nothing awaits him and his world has shrunk to the size of the mental space over which he and his new wife are continually wrangling.

The fifth and last sequence opens with the situation continuing to contract upon return to Shanghai. Differences in family background exacerbate the basic lack of harmony between Hongjian and Roujia. The Fang's continue to try and uphold the old values of their vanishing class, in spite of the straitened circumstances in the "isolated island" of 1939 Shanghai, a city maintaining a precarious existence under the condominium rule of foreign powers while totally surrounded by Japanese-occupied territory. They expect Roujia to observe a variety of ceremonies which, coming from a Westernized nuclear family, she does not even understand. The Suns' are likewise intolerant of the Fangs' empty posturing. Like every other element of the last sequence, this situation is parallel to a set of relationships that had been developed in the first part of the book. In this case, the relationship between the Fangs' and Suns' is a variation of that between the Fangs' and Zhous'. The difference is that in each episode of the ninth chapter, bills past due are called in: the free relationships that had seemed without consequence in the second and third chapters are recapitulated at the end, with their full range of overtone and implication revealed to us at last.[7] Similarly, the aunt for whom Roujia works and who pays her twice that salary that Hongjian is able to obtain at his meager journalistic job is a harder image of the comprador family of the second chapter. This time, however, Hongjian's life is within range of being affected by such people; he can no longer have dinner and run away. By the final chapter, in other words, the easy contempt which his breeding had instilled in him—and transmitted to the narrative tone—has become a helpless rage. And at the very end, with the final break between Hongjian and Roujia, the narrator takes full control of the point of view to show the futility of Hongjian's situation and any possible attitude that he could adopt toward it.

The course of the novel's transformation from somewhat facile satire to true pathos carries the major burden of shocking the reader into awareness—always a major purpose of Qian's creative writing. The implications of such a desire to shock will be described hereafter, but if the hypothesis of transformation of narrative mode is correct, some explanation of how such a difficult process is accomplished is in order. Such shifts in tones are often regarded as fatal to the overall structure of the work in which they are contained,[8] and many contemporary Chinese critics in fact noticed the phenomenon in *Wei Cheng* and viewed it as symptomatic of the novel's lack of structural integrity.[9] Wayne Booth touches on the theoretical problem involved in his discussion of Joyce's *Stephen Hero:*

If [Joyce] treats the author-figure [i.e., the character in the novel] satirically, as he does in much of *Stephen Hero*, . . . then what happens to the qualities of the epiphanies *he* [i.e., Stephen] describes? Are they still genuine epiphanies or only what the misguided, callow youth *thinks* are epiphanies? If, as Joyce's brother Stanislaus has revealed, the word "hero" is satire, can we take seriously the anti-hero's vision? Yet if the satirical mode is dropped, if the hero is made into a real hero, and if the reader is made to see things entirely as he sees them, what then happens to objectivity? The portrait is no longer an objective rendering of reality, looked at from respectable aesthetic distance, but rather a mere subjective indulgence.[10]

The problem in *Fortress* is similar: how to balance a far-ranging and merciless satire against the need for identification with character which is the essence of tragedy. This balance must be effected without, on the one hand, removing the narrative so far from the main character as to leave the reader unsympathetic to his plight[11]—as had been too often the situation in Qian's short stories—or, on the other hand, allowing us so close to him that we wallow together with him in his despair without obtaining any overall vision of its significance. The latter situation is prevalent in a good many modern Chinese novels of what Leo Lee has identified as the "romantic" type; Ba Jin is perhaps the writer most given to thus indulging his protagonists.

The uniqueness of *Fortress Besieged* lies just in its ability to bridge this gap between the subjective and the objective, to give a clear representation of a *sense* of absolute objectivity and then effectively to cut the ground out from under it by showing us how our perceptions have been shaped by what has been all along an errant subjectivity. The difference between the two visions allows the reader both to sympathize with the deluded Fang and to gain a clear perspective on his predicament. The structural key to this achievement is Qian's skillful manipulation of point of view. The contrast between investing the narrative center of consciousness in and withdrawing it from the mind of Fang Hongjian mirrors the dual approach to reality. Since the vast majority of the narrative is told from his standpoint, with frequent recourse to interior and narrated monologue, the textual problem is less one of engendering reader identification with him than of establishing a legitimate voice aside from his.

Qian does this, almost subliminally, and in a manner harkening back to his earlier prose, by setting up a series of mood frames at various points in the novel. These serve to establish the basis for a strong narrator's voice, in spite of its relative infrequency of appearance. At least in the first half of the novel, this separate voice is formally distinct by virtue of its extreme elaborateness of diction, both from the more straightforward narrative centered on Fang and from the dialogue. The highly decorative, allusive, and imagistic prose of the essays comes to be the property of this narrative voice. In a few broad strokes, this voice, which generally takes over at transitional points in the narrative, can set the stage for a whole sequence or, as in the passage to follow, the whole book. Its most salient feature is that it far surpasses the ability of any character, particularly Fang Hongjian, to perceive the vector that events will form themselves into.

Sequence One: In Shanghai

The novel's opening two paragraphs, while more eloquent than most, are characteristic of this omniscient mode of narration:

> With the Red Sea far behind, the ship navigated the Indian Ocean. But the sun still unforgivingly set late and rose early, encroaching upon the better part of the night. The night, like oil-stained paper, had become semi-translucent; it had been firmly embraced by the sun and was unable to extricate itself—perhaps the sun had intoxicated it. So even after the departure of the illuminated clouds of late evening, the night had a slightly flushed appearance. When the flush of evening dissipated and the stupor was over, the people sleeping in their cabins, bodies covered with sweat, awoke, bathed and hurried up on deck to breathe the sea air: another day had begun. This was the end of July, according with the "dog days" of the Chinese calendar, the hottest time of the year. In China, the heat was even more severe than usual; afterwards people all said it was a sign of war, for this was 1937.
> The French packet, the *Vicomte de Bragelonne,* was sailing for China. In the morning at eight, the just-washed and not yet quite dry third class deck was filled with standing or sitting people—Frenchmen, Jews fleeing Germany, Indians, Annamese and, needless to say, Chinese. The morning sea wind already carried a baking heat, and a sere wind blew dry the bodies of fat people; they were covered by a layer of salt-sweat frost, as if they had just bathed in the Dead Sea. But it was, after all, early morning, and people's enthusiasm had yet to be withered or roasted into laziness by the sun; speech and action both were lively. The French policemen being sent to Annam or to the French concessions in China surrounded the coquettish Jewish woman, flirting with her. Bismarck once remarked that the outstanding characteristic of French ambassadors and ministers abroad was their inability to speak one word of a foreign tongue. These policemen, not understanding German at all, but still able to get their feelings across and cause the woman to giggle, thus far surpassed their diplomats. The woman's good-looking husband sat to one side in amusement, as he had been the recipient of not a few cigarettes, beers and lemonades over the past few days. The Red Sea was behind, so there was no more fear of intense heat igniting

a fire; thus, momentarily, the deck would be completely covered with a litter of fruit skins, paper, bottle caps and cigarette butts as well. The French are renowned for their lucidity of thought and their writing is clean and clear, but in action they are nothing if not confused, dirty and raucous: one need look no farther than the chaos on the boat. The boat, relying on human skill, was loaded with human disorder, invested with human hope. With every moment of its boisterous course, it returned a small square of humanity-corrupted water to the unfeeling, unending, unbounded ocean.[12]

A notable point of this passage is its lack of narrative movement: paradoxically, in view of the fact that the ship is in motion, the words paint a strictly fixed picture of the boat. The reiteration of the concept of heat and its effects continually reinforces this stasis and clearly filiates it with the "baroque style" of the essays. The last sentence of the first paragraph and the last two sentences of the second, moreover, encapsulate the irony and change of mood which characterized transitions in the essays. The end of paragraph one jolts us out of the petty concern with the discomfort of heat by reminding us of its relationship to the ongoing course of contemporary history, while the end of the second paragraph throws a retrospective somberness over the whole of man's relationship with nature, echoing the theme of "God's Dream." The sudden evocation of this immensity and impassivity turns the contrast between humans and their natural discomfort in summer—a temporary condition, after all—into a general and unforgiving principle. A comparison with Hardy's pessimistic view of the relationship between man and nature will demonstrate the bleakness of Qian's vision. In a passage which similarly sets the mood for *The Mayor of Casterbridge,* Hardy writes:

The difference between the peacefulness of inferior nature and the willful hostilities of mankind was very apparent at this place. . . . In presence of this scene . . . there was a natural instinct to abjure man as the blot on an otherwise kindly universe: till it was remembered that all terrestrial conditions were intermittent, and that mankind might some night be innocently sleeping when these quiet objects were raging loud.[13]

At least Hardy is willing to concede separate existences to humans and nature and the fact that they do not necessarily corrupt one another. Qian, however, in the last sentence of the passage, makes clear that nature is a latent force that can only be potentiated by interaction with humans; the plain implication is that the interaction is invariably hostile. Thus, in one of his finest ironies, Qian displays the dark side of one of the most basic tenets of traditional Chinese poetics: the union between subjective feeling *(qing)* and outer reality *(jing)*.[14] It becomes an inextricable encumbrance which offers no hope of grace or of the separation out and positive employment of human will.

Qian does not, however, maintain this high seriousness of tone for long. The following passage describes the Chinese students aboard ship:

As usual each summer, a batch of Chinese students was returning home upon completing their studies. There were about a dozen on this ship, most of whom were young and as yet without occupation. By hurrying back to China at the beginning of the summer vacation, they could leisurely look for jobs. Students who did not need to worry about not having jobs could wait for the autumn cool before gradually setting off for home. These aboard the boat, who had studied in such places as France, England, Germany and Belgium, had all been to Paris for a taste of night life and hence were taking a French boat back. Meeting at the ends of the earth, they became old friends immediately; they talked of the internal and external threats to the homeland and wished they could be there instantaneously in order to be of service. But the ship moved so slowly, and with everyone pining away fruitlessly with no outlet for their feelings, suddenly two sets of mahjong tiles appeared out of nowhere. Mahjong, of course, aside from being the national sport, was also reputed to be popular in America. Playing mahjong thus not only possessed the flavor of home but was in accord with international fashion. (2/4)

This is a *chedan* identical to any in the essays, with the gravity of the initial exposition radically diluted. In the novel, however, such transformations from serious to flippant mood are structurally important in terms of ultimate narrative development. Because these two types of voice are the *only* two narrative modes in the story, their alternation is the key to setting up the distinction between the limited vision of Fang and the extensive right to knowledge which is the property of the omniscient narrator.

A dour passage also marks the beginning of the third chapter:

> Perhaps because so many people had died in battle, the spent life forces of those who had been killed unjustly contributed to the burgeoning of spring. That spring, the weather was extraordinarily good. The aura of spring stimulated people's hearts like the gums of a teething baby feeling the itch of organic budding. Shanghai is a parvenu city; it has no landscapes and gardens in which to lodge spring—the plants in private gardens and parks were like animals shut up in the zoo: restrained, lonely, not able to give full outlet to the spring light. When spring came it could only invest itself in human hearts and minds. It increased sickness and contagion, increased rape and drunken brawling, increased pregnancies. The last was not, after all, a bad thing; population should be replaced during a war. But according to Mrs. Zhou, most of the children born this year were the spirits of those who had died unjustly. Their time on earth not being complete, they had found their way to conception in order to live out their alloted spans; they would thus probably not live long. (43/48)

This passage begins in typical "baroque style" by dilating upon various facets of the opening statement. It also harkens to and cannibalizes a common trope in Chinese literature, that of the quickening of human feeling engendered by spring, and deliberately turns it on its head. Instead, however, of the arbitrary overturning of traditional motifs by linguistic fiat that marked the undermining process of the essays, the dashing of traditional sensibility here is accomplished by linking the description to the historical process that is going on all around.

The connection of the irony of the times with the irony of the composition reaches its height with the description of spring's part in increasing sickness and violence. Underlying this irony is the further unhappy juxtaposition between spring and the city. The concluding section on metempsychosis is both a *chedan* and an underscoring of human incapacity to deal with this concatenation of forces. The uniqueness, power and asperity of the images reflect the almost divine powers that the narrator arrogates to himself. He is divine not only in that he is arbitrary, ever-present and omnipotent but also in his deliberate keeping out of sight most of the time.[15] Insofar as the employment of arresting images marks the strength of the omniscient narrator's voice, the force and reason behind the display of such new and brilliant metaphor is explained by F. O. Matthiessen when he observes that "only by discovering such metaphors can the writer suggest the actual complexity of experience; and consequently, the more of them he is able to perceive, the more comprehensive is his grasp of human life."[16]

In contrast to this narrative omnipotence and omniscience, the scenes observed through Hongjian partake of his particular mood at the time of narration. In the first part of the book, therefore, the tone is predominantly frivolous. There are numerous ways in which narrative consciousness is focused in Fang's mind; the principal and most obvious of these is that almost every scene contains him as either the pivot around whom the action centers or the reflector of opinion concerning the course of action that is going on before him.[17] The unity between Hongjian and narrative voice is apparent in the following passage, which takes place just after his return to Shanghai. He and the Zhous' are discussing his marriage prospects:

Mother-in-law said: "Hongjian just isn't crafty enough to find a girl for himself. How about my being matchmaker?"

Father-in-law said: "There you go again. Don't you think his own father and mother will be able to handle the situation? It's none of our business."

Mother-in-law said: "The money that Hongjian used to go overseas was ours, so when he picks a wife he can't just leave us out of it, isn't that so, Hongjian? Your new wife will have to be my *gannüer*. I'll tell you this straight to your face; don't forget your old family when you find a new one! I've seen all sorts of heartless people like that."

Hongjian could only laugh bitterly and say: "Don't worry, that won't happen." [But] he said silently to Miss Su's shadow: "Listen to this! Are you willing to have this woman as your *ganma?* You're lucky I don't want to marry you." His young "brother-in-law" picked up on his thoughts and said: "Hongjian, there's a woman who studied overseas named Su, do you know her?" Hongjian was so startled that his ricebowl almost dropped from his hands; he thought that American behavioral scientists had only proved that "thought is another language," so what was the structure of this fellow's ears, that even this secret and soundless language of his mind was completely overheard! (27/30)[18]

The initial, short conversation adequately establishes the crudity of Mrs. Zhou, but Hongjian's mental commentary has the effect that we have seen in Qian's stories: it seems to come from a narrator who does not quite trust his reader to perceive what is already quite apparent. In *Fortress* this type of commentary is most often supplied by Hongjian rather than by the omniscient voice. Furthermore, the description of Hongjian's reaction to his "brother-in-law's" question is marked by the sort of erudite free association that I have described as being the principal indicator of the narrator's voice. Here the insertion of the word "thought" obviously places it in Hongjian's mind. This frequent overlapping between the narrative voice and Fang's presence on the scene predisposes the reader to think of them as being one. The lack of person indicators in Chinese verbs heightens this ambiguity. With the narrative thus following Hongjian's movements and thoughts and possessing the same tone as his mood of the moment, the reader comes to accept him as the agency through which events occur.

As the story meanders along at Fang's pace, however, with this ambiguity of voice clouding any sense of real narrative movement, there are sudden points within it at which the other two structural elements of the text—mimetic dialogue and the omnipotent narrator—rise up and take over. At these junctures, they completely efface the identification between Fang and narrator as well as any illusion that Hongjian is in command of events. At such points Fang's assorted mistakes are added up and their consequences made clear. One such narrative crisis point is the climactic meeting between Hongjian and Tang Xiaofu. He had just summoned the courage to break with Su Wenwan, and a few days later he goes to see Tang with a marriage proposal. In the meantime, however, Su had gone to see Tang and told her, with embellishment, of certain indiscretions in Fang's past. These indiscretions have all been depicted in the course of the narrative, but as the audience has seen them from Hongjian's viewpoint, it has either been cajoled into forgiving him or has come to see them as mere fripperies because of the frivolous mood in which they were undertaken. Tang Xiaofu, however, is not so complaisant, and the fury of her response causes the reader to reexamine his own reactions to the same events:

Hongjian braved the rain to go to the Tangs'; the young lady, to his surprise, was home. He vaguely noticed that the servant's attitude was a bit peculiar, but paid no attention. As soon as he saw Miss Tang, he realized that today she was extraordinarily reserved and without a trace of her usual smile; she came out clutching a large paper package. His bravery totally dissolved, and he said: "I came by twice, but you weren't home. Did you receive the letter I sent Monday?"

"I received it, Mr. Fang"—Hongjian heard her return to her original form of address and did not dare to breathe—"I heard that Mr. Fang also came by on Tuesday; why didn't you come in? I was home that day."

"Miss Tang"—he also returned to his original form of address—"how did you know I came by on Tuesday?"

"My cousin's driver saw you and wondered why you passed by without dropping in; he told my cousin and my cousin told me. You should have come in that day; it so happens that we were talking about you."

"What is there to say about somebody like me?"

"We were not only talking about you, you might say we were studying you. We decided that your actions are quite mysterious."

"How can I be mysterious?"

"Not mysterious? Of course we're not sophisticated people and have no idea of such higher subtleties. I have always known you can talk well, so you must have a very complete and satisfying explanation of what you have done. At least when you say, 'I have no excuse, there is no way that I can explain,' everyone will certainly forgive you. Am I not correct?"

"What?" Hongjian took a start. "Did you see the letter I wrote your cousin?"

"My cousin showed it to me; moreover, she gave me a complete account of events from your time on the boat until the other night [when Hongjian had, more or less involuntarily, kissed Su; the next day he had written her the letter referred to, telling her the whole thing had been a misunderstanding]."

The anger on Miss Tang's face increased; Hongjian did not dare to look her in the eye.

"What did she say?" Hongjian asked haltingly: he was sure that Su Wenwan had exaggerated her account, had said that he had led her on, then kissed her; he prepared to answer back with the facts.

"You mean you don't even know what you yourself did?"

"Miss Tang, let me explain—"

"If you have 'a way to explain,' first go tell it to my cousin." Ordinarily Fang Hongjian loved Miss Tang's intelligence, but now he wished only that she were a dullard and not so overbearing. "My cousin also told me a few things about you and I don't know whether they are correct or not. You are now living with the Zhous', who, I hear, are not just ordinary relatives but are your in-laws. I understand that you have married"—Hongjian wanted to interrupt, but Miss Tang was after all a lawyer's daughter and knew the secret of interrogating a witness: do not allow him to argue back— "I don't need an explanation. Are they your in-laws or not? If they are, that's that. I don't know whether or not you had any girl friends while you were abroad all those years, but on your way home you took a fancy to one Miss Bao and you hit it off so well you became constant companions, right?" Hongjian lowered his head and said nothing. "After Miss Bao left, you pursued my cousin, right up until—well, I really don't need to go on. Furthermore, I hear that when you were in Europe studying you received an American degree—"

Hongjain stamped his foot and said harshly: "Did I ever brag to you about having a degree? That was all a joke."

"You're so intelligent that you have a trick for every occasion, but simple folk like me take your jokes for the real thing"—Miss Tang had heard Fang Hongjian's throat catch and she weakened; but by this time, the more she felt sorry for him, the more she hated him and the more she wished to punish him—"Mr. Fang, your past is too rich for my taste. I want to occupy the whole life of the person I love; before meeting me he should have nothing but a blank waiting for me to fill"—Hongjian still had his head soundlessly lowered—"I can only wish you a glorious future."

Hongjian was numb body and soul, as if electrified; he knew only that Miss Tang was speaking about him, but he was in no state really to listen to what she was saying. It was as if his brain were covered with a layer of oiled paper: her words, like rain drops, did not sink in.

But the oiled paper shivered under the weight of the rain drops. He had heard the last sentence and forlornly understood; he raised his head and his eyes were filled with tears; like that of a big child who had been scolded and beaten, it was a face showing pent-up hurt. Miss Tang suddenly felt as if she too would cry. "Everything you said is true. I'm a fraud, I won't dare to try and argue anymore. From now on I won't bother you any more." He stood up to go.

Miss Tang wished she could say: "Why don't you defend yourself ? I would believe you," but she said only: "Goodbye then." She accompanied him to the door, wishing that he would say something. Outside it was raining hard, and when they reached the door she hoped he would stay until the rain slackened a little. Hongjian put on his raincoat, looked at Miss Tang and was afraid to shake her hand. Miss Tang saw the light in his eyes, brightened by the burst of tears; she lowered her own eyes, not being able to bear to look any longer. She mechanically put out her hand and said, "Goodbye"—sometimes "Won't you stay a little longer" can force people to leave and sometimes "Goodbye" can induce people to stay; but Miss Tang could not induce Fang Hongjian to stay, so she added, "I hope your journey to the interior is pleasant." She returned to her room, tired and vexed, her great rage all gone. (102–104/*102–104*)

This scene, which links the first series of causalities and rings them down on Hongjian, begins in the fashion of the majority of the narrative: we see it through Fang's eyes. In the first few sentences the reader's perceptions are those we share with him. In the dialogue sequence which follows, however, Hongjian is given no opportunity to filter the situation through his consciousness and thus maneuver it, and the narrative, back under his control. His one attempt at recouping—when he asks Tang what her cousin had said—is summarily rebuffed. When Tang Xiaofu reaches her account of Miss Bao, Fang is speechless (and thoughtless). As her verbal battering continues, the power of reflecting events that had been invested in Hongjian is gradually withdrawn. The final shock of hearing Miss Bao's name reduces him to numbness and the narrative to description strictly exterior to Fang. It is as if—under the carefree progress of the narrative to which Fang introduces us—there runs another, harsher tale, controlled by events outside the range of his mentality.

One indicator of this is the reemergence of the omniscient narrator, who reasserts his powerful voice at this juncture to give us a carefully balanced account of the actions and feelings of both characters; another indicator is the fact that this narrator exerts his control here by means of showing us a side of Miss Tang that we have not seen before. She has heretofore always been seen by us through the eyes of Hongjian, and we have thus seen only a happy and compliant person. Only when events conjoin like this and Fang's ability to manipulate reality breaks down are we given a real opportunity to see that she has a viewpoint of her own. And her viewpoint is not only uncongenial to his on many issues, but it is also shown to be—through the disjointed dialogue and his failure to see her real intentions—fundamentally beyond his ken. Person and person—like person and world—are thereby demonstrated to be, at root, antipathetic to one another. And what Fang learns through such adversity merely sums up retrospectively a series of past mistakes without providing any new means to deal with an ever more hostile future.

The points where the narrative withdraws from Hongjian's viewpoint, then, are the novelistic equivalent of the shocking concluding statements in the essays. These changes in viewpoint also serve to give us glimpses into the basic dispositions of the characters in *Fortress* other than Fang Hongjian. With the narrative primarily satirical and centered on Fang, there would be a natural tendency for the other characters to become caricatures. Indeed, at most times the other characters do appear as stereotypes. In saying this, however, it would be well to keep in mind one of the statements Melville makes on the craft of fiction in *The Confidence Man:* "That fiction, where every character can, by reason of its consistency, be comprehended at a glance, either exhibits but sections of character, making them appear for wholes, or else is very untrue to reality."[19] A true representation of Hongjian *and* his perceptual world requires that we see the other characters as he does; he necessarily only sees part and takes them for wholes, and the reader must be led to appreciate fully the reality of this perception. The final meaning of the novel is surely the demonstration of how the alienation which a corrupt world brings about is manifested in everyone. If Fang were not partially aware of this, and if he did not possess the jaundiced view of the characters which float past him that such alienation implies, we would lose interest in him. At the same time, however, the depiction of the essential nature of such a society requires that the true power relations within it be made clear, and these relations must remain hidden from Fang for him to function as heedlessly as he does through most of the book. The force of the novel depends, in fact, on the disharmony the reader perceives between the absurdity or incomprehensibility of the actors and the very real consequences that they bring about.

The tension between these two phenomena is, as described by Scholes and Kellogg, part of the natural process of the development of fictional "realism" or, to put the matter somewhat more analytically, of fictions which problematically explore the distinctions and interactions between convention and contingency. As they say:

[S]atire naturally flourishes when the world is in transition from an ideally oriented moral scheme of the cosmos to an empirically oriented non-moral scheme. . . . [T]he validity of satire depends on its ability to convince the reader, at least temporarily, that the social and moral types of the real world are being represented more truly as caricatures than they had been in the idealizing art and thought to which the satire offers itself for comparison.

They note further that "the natural tendency is for satire to drift toward mimesis proper, the characters losing their status as generalized types and taking on the problematic qualities we associate with the novel."[20]

In this formulation, however, Scholes and Kellogg seem to take for granted a vivid contrast between old values and new; it would seem essential that "for satire to drift toward mimesis proper," a new society must emerge in which the author can make new and reasonable assumptions about human behavior and its motivation. What *Fortress* and Hongjian's disposition in it represent, however, is a society in which the old ways hang on, without making any sense, but where the shape of a new order from which these values can be confidently lampooned and transcended is yet to come into being. Thus Hongjian is forced, as it were, to conduct a personal satire within a highly problematic, "mimetic" situation—with tragic results.

The character of Fang himself, as it is first presented to us, then, demands a progression up from satire. I have already remarked on Hongjian's frivolity in the first section of the book (something the omniscient narrator makes much of when he introduces Fang on pp. 6–11/8–15). This superficiality, however, comes to be superseded by a persistent self-effacement that matches his critical attitude toward others: he almost becomes a caricature in his own eyes. This attitude is introduced in the capsule description which follows his entry into the narrative, when it recounts the self-contempt he feels on buying a diploma. This sense of his own fraudulence is easily transferred to others, often in ways which compound his own feelings of unworthiness. For instance, when the ship from Europe docks in Shanghai, his brother Pengtu meets him and sees Su Wenwan tell Hongjian goodbye: "Pengtu asked who it was and Hongjian said that her name was Su. Pengtu said: 'Oh, that's the Ph.D. from France I read about in the papers.' Hongjian laughed coldly and thought uncharitably about female vanity" (26/29). That very evening, however, in the same conversation with the Zhous' partially translated above, they show him a newspaper in which the news of his "doctorate" that they had submitted had been published. His response is a narrated monologue which plainly shows his own low self-esteem:

And at the time he had thought she was common! But this news about him was really the very pit of vulgarity; it stank so that readers would have to hold their noses. Plus the fact that she was a real Ph.D.: what did that make him? On the ship he had not mentioned having a degree to Miss Su, so when she saw this she would surely think that he was trying to put one over. . . . So he had become a fraud; from now on how would he be able to look people in the eye? (28/31).

Seeing himself from this perspective, it is no wonder that he has nothing to say when Tang Xiaofu makes her accusations against him. But this negativism would not enable us to develop any real empathy with him if it were sustained in the same manner throughout the novel. It is the same mood which distances the reader from the characters in "Souvenir," and it must somehow be overcome if the novel is to involve the reader fully.

Sequence Two: The Journey

Qian begins to deal with this problem by temporarily placing Fang in a situation where convention exercises minimal restraint, this being the picaresque journey to the interior which comprises the second sequence. The lack of conventional rules on the trip obliges Hongjian to shape his own world and face the consequences in a qualitatively different manner than he would have if he had stayed in Shanghai and been allowed to drift within old custom. Were Hongjian still to face this new situation alone and contemptuously, however, the narrative upshot could still be simple satire. Even more important than the change of scene, then, is the entrance into the story of a character that Hongjian can seriously consider his equal—Zhao Xinmei. Zhao originally appeared as a member of Su Wenwan's salon, her ardent pursuer, and as a pompous ass. With Su's marriage to another, which diminishes Zhao's antipathy toward Fang, the process of planning the trip to Hunan brings the two men closer together.

The closeness between these two, which lasts, in varying degrees, until the end of the novel, finally provides a parallel character by whom we can gain the real measure of Fang.[21] Hongjian no longer exists in a world of shades but now has someone, circumstantially very much like him, through whom there develops a series of comparisons and contrasts which add dimension to Fang's character. The dialogues on a variety of subjects that they have while on the road add a degree of mental reflection on events going by that theretofore had almost been the exclusive province of the omniscient narrator. These conversations provide the transition to the representation of Fang as a serious and thoughtful person. Indeed, as the novel progresses, Hongjian takes on more of the pessimism of the omniscient voice, without, of course, taking on any of its ability to control the unfolding of events. Fang, if only after the fact, learns from his misfortunes and approaches a rounded view of his predicament, paradoxically in inverse proportion to his ability to do anything about it.

Just as this friendship is on the point of developing, however, the first part of a mood frame is established which tells the careful reader of a fundamental difference between Fang and Zhao, one that does not surface on the trip but becomes increasingly prominent thereafter. The passage in which this is set forth is another example of Qian's setting the ground of consequence in a way so subtle as to be almost subliminal. It occurs as Hongjian is on the way to Xinmei's apartment to be told about the specifics of the arrangements at Sanlü:

At just five o'clock Fang Hongjian found Zhao Xinmei's foreign-style apartment; as he went in the door he heard that a number of the flats had their radios on and tuned to a broadcast of the current hit: "Spring Love Song"; the air was shattered by the sharp voice of the locally produced superstar singer. . . . Reaching Zhao's door on the second floor he heard the broadcast issuing from there as well. He rang the bell and thought, What in hell! Listening to this sort of song is like looking at pornographic books or pictures—an indication of lack of intelligence and neurosis—he had not expected Zhao Xinmei to have sunk so low from disappointment in love! (120–121/22–23)

The elided portion is essentially a *chedan* mocking the song and the singer through a series of word plays. It lightens the mood and has the effect of distracting our attention from the following section, in which Hongjian discovers Xinmei listening to such vulgar music.

There is, however, a serious symbolism in this section. Entering that door determines the way in which Fang goes to the interior as well as beginning his friendship with Zhao. The combination of these two actions, in turn, determines the way in which he arrives at the university, or, in essence, the whole downward course on which he is about to embark. Seen in retrospect, going through that door represents a major step in the necessary and practical compromise of his principles—principles which at any rate have done nothing to that point but cause inaction and a supercilious disregard for others. Now, however, by joining people who listen to such songs, Fang determines himself to participation in society on their own terms. Just as he begins at last to take someone else seriously, the reader is made to perceive that a gulf remains that can never close.

Fang, however, if he ever paid much attention to it in the first place, soon forgets this episode in the course of preparations for and the beginning of the journey itself. Fang and Zhao get along famously, the social constraints of the fixed society from which they had come forgotten between the two of them. And in spite of their fears of being trapped into marriage, they get along passably well with the younger Sun Roujia as well. Li Meiting and Gu Erqian, however, serve as constant reminders of the corruption of the society from which they have come and foreshadow the corruption which lies ahead.

The hopefulness of the start that youth could create if unencumbered by convention is represented in the one leg of the journey where the younger three have become separated from Li and Gu and spend the evening together at an inn (pp. 152–52/ 156–57). It is the one episode of the trip sequence where no fights break out and no tempers fray. As soon as Li and Gu are present, though, the situation becomes fraught with tension. Hongjian, in spite of the need the journey imposes of creating a new world of relationships and personal responsibilities, cannot rid himself of the sense of degradation brought on by such company: "When he could not sleep at night, Hongjian felt sorry for himself; the more he thought about it, the more he regretted having come along. Being in the same party as Li Meiting and Gu Erqian was shameful degeneracy" (165/170). As the trip goes on, therefore, Fang is more and more unable to stifle his chronic discontent; he loses no opportunity to pick at Li verbally and does little but complain. His helplessness reaches a peak when the group reaches Jian, where they are to pick up supplementary travel funds which the school has wired them. Upon reaching the town, they find that the money has indeed been sent, but that they need a guarantor in order to receive it from the bank. After Zhao, Li and Gu have exhausted all avenues (Hongjian cannot go along because his physical appearance during the course of the trip has declined more than that of the others), Gu makes the suggestion that Roujia go to the Women's Association and try her luck there.

Fang's immediate response to this suggestion is, to say the least, unhelpful: "Fang Hongjian utilized his knowledge of psychology and said: 'It won't do any good to go. Women are suspicious by nature, and petty. Send a woman to ask something of another woman and you'll run up against a brick wall' " (176/ 183). When Roujia is gone for some time, Hongjian is the first to give up hope. Much to his surprise, however, Roujia succeeds in finding a guarantor at the Association. At the celebration banquet, Hongjian thus announces to everyone that " 'I'm really ashamed, I didn't contribute anything to this effort; I'm just a good-for-nothing,' " to which Li replies, with one of the few just remarks he is to make in the entire novel: " 'That's right. Fang's a real lord, sits in the hotel and doesn't make a move while we run around for him. Xinmei, even though our efforts were in vain, we did put a lot into trying, right?' " (178/185). While the reader's perception of events is still almost exclusively funneled through Fang in this sequence, so that we see the justice of most of the young man's complaints, we must also admit the truth of Li's remarks.

Nonetheless, we are not fully prepared, as we had not been fully prepared for the harsh objectivity of Tang's rebuff of Fang, for Zhao Xinmei's equally harsh assessment of Hongjian at the end of the chapter. As they walk beside the sedan chairs which are their means of transportation on the last leg of the trip to the school, Xinmei begins to sum up accurately the significance of the trip in terms of character development: " 'A trip like this one of ours is the best way of testing character. Travel is so tiring and obnoxious that it forces everyone's true nature out into the open. People who've undergone a difficult journey together and still don't hate each other can become real friends. . . .' " After some banter, Hongjian becomes serious again:

"Stop joking around. Let me ask you, now that this trip is over, what's your impression of me? Am I obnoxious or not?"

"You're not obnoxious, but you're completely useless."
Hongjian had not anticipated that Xinmei would reply this frankly and was so angry that he could only utter a bitter laugh. His enthusiasm for further conversation was spent and, after silently walking on a few more steps, he waved at Xinmei and said: "I'm getting back in the chair." He climbed into the chair and was melancholy; he did not understand why speaking plainly was considered a virtue. (183–184/ 190–91)

The sequence closes by completing the mood frame that had begun at the chapter's start with Hongjian's confession of a lack of enthusiasm for the journey. Once again, the unpromising beginning links up with the rude ending to give a version of the consequences of Hongjian's actions other than the one we had seen through Hongjian himself: his halfhearted participation is revealed as having been an obvious impediment to others rather than just some self-possessed existential anxiety. Again, he learns only after the events are passed and beyond remedy. The chance he had of acting on them in such a way as to suit both himself and the external world—if it ever existed—proves itself beyond Fang even in the situation where it is theoretically the most possible.

During the course of the journey Hongjian imperceptibly and unconsciously has begun to trade his closeness to Xinmei for a common sympathy with Roujia. This results from a series of circumstances over which he has no control, symbolized by one episode which takes place on the night before the arrival of the party at Sanlü. Encamped near an old graveyard, both Hongjian and Roujia are startled into wakefulness by identical dreams of the ghosts of children pulling at them. The next day they go to the graveyard to discuss the matter; Xinmei catches them talking and, in a sense, his observing them ratifies their closeness:

"What did you two come to this boneyard so early in the morning to talk about?" They told him of the events of the night before; he snorted and said: "Your souls are even united in your dreams, that's really something. But I didn't sense a thing myself; then, of course, I'm a coarse fellow and ghosts wouldn't deign to visit me. . . ." (183/190)

This new relationship, therefore, is hardly the result of any positive decision; it is not even based on anything as concrete as the common interests that Hongjian and Xinmei shared at the beginning of the trip. Its basic hollowness is indicated in Fang's musings about what the school will be like, contained in the passage that follows the one translated above. The dreams and musings fuse to form a mood frame which sets the tone for the third sequence—the account of life at Sanlü University:

> While riding in the sedan chair Hongjian wondered what it would be like when they arrived today at the school. At any rate, he was not holding on to any extravagant hopes. The broken-down facade that stood behind where they had spent the night was a good symbol. It seemed as though it were an entrance and that behind it there would be a great building, but when it had enticed you through, it revealed that there was nothing there; an entrance giving entry onto nothing, a place that goes no place. "Abandon all hope, ye who enter here." Although this was all true, he could not stifle a curiosity and hope that was like water boiling on a stove—it kept bubbling up to lift the pot's lid. (183/*190*)

As in "God's Dream," these events illustrate the emptiness of the symbols of mysticism. Fang's disposition is similarly one of futility: like that with which he began the trip, it virtually guarantees an inability to accommodate successfully to reality.

Sequence Three: At Sanlü

If the trip was a chance for Hongjian to forge a new world and world view outside the fixed bounds of bourgeois society which he could not take advantage of, the sequence at Sanlü represents the power of social convention redoubled. Consequences come rapidly and arbitrarily, and there is no way to avoid them. The full force of these new circumstances is brought home by a change in narrative mode. As will be remembered, in the first sequence, Hongjian, for all his laxity and for all the intolerance he encounters, appears as potentially a free agent. The narrative mode which reflected this condition had Fang as the center of consciousness and constructed itself from the series of his intentional acts. Thus, although he loses Tang Xiaofu, we see how the situation could have been otherwise, had Hongjian decided to act in different ways at certain key junctures in the text. The omniscient narrator intrudes only when Hongjian has failed to put together a series of self-consistent actions.

In the second sequence Fang makes a definite commitment to a group, which of course limits his ability to formulate his own fate, but, to the extent that the group is a free entity, he is potentially able to make a significant contribution to its fate. Had he done so, in other words, he would have been spared the barb of Zhao's final assessment and the dissonance between his personal viewpoint and that of external reality that the barb implies. The modal reflection of Fang's radically decreased opportunities upon arrival at Sanlü is a more objective narrative presentation of ongoing events, in which Hongjian's lack of control over his own fate is evident. Rather than dictating the general course of events, as in the first sequence, his actions are revealed to be working at cross-purposes to developments even as they are going on. His reflections on the action become mere commentary, and sometimes not even very accurate, at that.

In the third sequence, then, Fang's tentative commitment to positive action—lukewarm and contradictory though it may be—combines with the reinstitution of an oppressive social morality to render him incapable either of effective action or of simply shrugging things off. In this sequence, for the first time, the omniscient narrative voice separates itself from Hongjian's perceptual field for relatively long periods to unfold events. From the beginning of the sixth chapter, the reader is given glimpses into the thought processes of other characters (on page 186/194–95, for instance, there is even an internal monologue—the first by any character other than Hongjian—issuing from Gao Songnian, the president of the university), and long stretches of the action take place without Fang on the scene at all. (During the scene-setting for the matchmaking dinner to which Hongjian and Xinmei are invited {229–35/239–44}, for example, Fang does not appear. This is his longest absence from the narrative since he was introduced on page 6/8.) Thus the "real"narrative, that veritable record of cause and effect which was mostly hidden from Hongjian and the reader in the first two sequences, now goes on quite openly. It comprises the machinations and intrigues which whirl through the "school for scandal" that is Sanlü.

Had Hongjian known of the existence of this causality in the first five chapters, it would have been quite within range of his capabilities to alter it (the problem, of course, was involved with the very process of knowing). But the infinite set of possibilities that was open to him at the beginning of the story has exhausted itself, and his new knowledge is useless. For example, the proximate cause of the train of events which leads to his dismissal is Xinmei's involvement with a faculty wife, a situation over which Hongjian has no control, in spite of the fact that he knows about it. It is in the third sequence, then, that Fang trades the ability to maneuver reality for an increasing ability to see clearly what it is that is happening to him. And like all things governed by the fable of the besieged city, the trade of one thing for the other represents no gain for the character involved.

This is also the sequence in which the person to whom Hongjian is closest changes decisively from Xinmei to Sun Roujia. But shifting confidants is not a matter of Hongjian's free choice: the difference between Hongjian's tenuous and Xinmei's secure positions has created a barrier between them, and the turn to Roujia is simply to the only one left in the maze in which he has involved himself. This initial glimmer of thinking of Roujia as someone to talk to gains force in Fang's mind, and when he hears a false rumor about her romantic involvement with another faculty member, his mixed feelings surprise him. When the rumor is demonstrated to be false and Roujia, in visiting him one day to ask him for advice, tells him that there are now rumors circulating about the two of them, Hongjian is thrown into a real quandary. After she leaves

Hongjian dejectedly fell into his chair; his body was intermittently hot and cold, as if he had malaria. What a mess, he thought. What could be the content of this gossip? When two people are together others are determined to start rumors, just as when two branches of a tree are adjacent a spider will make a web. Today he had just not been able to shut up, he had said a lot of things he needn't and shouldn't have said [i.e., in giving Roujia advice]. Wasn't this giving foundation to the gossip? . . . If he was to be responsible for her marriage, what would he do? Hongjian was so upset that he could neither sit nor stand; he roamed about the room. If he didn't love Miss Sun, then what did the gossip matter to him? Did he love her then—love her just a little? (252/262–63)

Fang's turning to Roujia as a friend, then, removes from his control the basic question of determining what sort of relationship there is to be between them. Social pressure is gradually taking over the disposition of the relationship.

The full import of this comes a few pages later when the two of them become engaged. Instead of being the result of serious consideration and decision, it is an on-the-spot announcement teased out of Hongjian when Li Meiting and another teacher catch them talking together:

Li Meiting smiled slyly and said: "You two really are caught up in your conversation; I called out a couple of times but you didn't even hear. I wanted to ask you when it was that Xinmei left—sorry to interrupt your sweet talk, Miss Sun."

Heedless of everything, Hongjian said: "If you knew it was 'sweet talk,' you shouldn't have interrupted."

Li Meiting said: "You two really are in the height of fashion, walking hand in hand in broad daylight. What a model for the students!"

Hongjian said: "Well, your model of paying visits to the village 'pleasure quarters' is beyond us."

Li Meiting blanched, but, finding a way to change the subject, he said: "You always have been a joker. Stop trying to evade [*chedan*] and be serious. When are you sending out the wedding invitations?"

Hongjian said: "When the time comes you won't be left out."

Miss Sun said hesitantly: "Then we're telling Mr. Li"—Li Meiting shouted and Lu Zixiao screeched: "Tell us what? About your engagement, right?"

Miss Sun merely grasped Hongjian more closely and did not reply. The other two continued their clamoring: "Congratulations! Congratulations, Miss Sun! Did he propose just today? You'll have to celebrate!" They forced the couple to shake hands with them and went on with their teasing.

Hongjian's head was as if in a cloud, with no autonomy to act. He let them shake his hand and pat him on the shoulder; only when he agreed to take them out and celebrate did they leave. Miss Sun waited until they were gone away and said apologetically: "I saw those two and panicked, I didn't know what to do. Please forgive me for what I just said, I didn't really mean it!"

Hongjian suddenly felt weary, body and soul; he had no energy to cope, so he grabbed her hand and said: "But I meant everything I said. Maybe it was just what I was going to ask."

Miss Sun was silent; after a good while she said: "I hope you won't regret this," and lifted her face waiting for a kiss. But he forgot about kissing her and said only: "I hope you'll have no regrets either." (264–65/275–76)

This episode completes the Sanlü sequence by summing up the new relationship of Fang to reality that has emerged in the sixth and seventh chapters. Entering the school, he was defined in terms of Zhao Xinmei, a friendship he had entered into freely and which symbolized a certain residual ability to shape his own environment. With his gradual estrangement from Xinmei, however, his ability to shape events alters accordingly. He becomes defined by a relationship to Roujia which came into being without any real free choice on his part. The key sentence in the passage above, which represents this situation, is the one which tells of his being "with no autonomy to act" when the critical moment comes. Thus this episode is also the opening of the mood frame for the fourth and final sequence. By this time, the narrative ceases to result at all from Fang's intentional acts and becomes instead a fragmented agglutination of the intentional acts of others and of the crush of impersonal events. The only character integrity that remains to him is the purely negative consciousness of denying both the designs of others and the pattern of the times. But this continual negation of external reality can only reduce to nothing his own sphere of being.

Sequence Four: Back to the City

The background for Fang's reduction in the final sequence is his return to urban China. With his thus coming full circle, he has gathered wisdom,[22] but with events having come full circle as well, they continue to elude his power to shape them. Many of the episodes in the eighth and ninth chapters, therefore, deliberately parallel episodes in the first through the third chapters; the contrast between them reveals the enormity of the change that has taken place. This repetition of events in a new context provides a constant measure with which to gauge the omniscient narrator's text against the text of Fang Hongjian. In this process, the dreary frame with which the novel opened is brought to a close and the book's meaning made clear.

In a monologue which provides a cadence for the eighth chapter and an introduction to the even more degrading events that await him in Shanghai, Hongjian achieves a measure of realization concerning the futility of his own past actions. The monologue is significant on a number of levels: it marks the growth of his self-knowledge as well as notifying the reader of a fundamental truth about Hongjian's position as an actuator of events. As it is also part of a conversation between Hongjian and Roujia on the significance of their imminent arrival in Shanghai, it represents a further step in the decline of their relationship as well. The monologue is occasioned by Roujia's contrast of the trip out with the trip in as being a manifestation of the power of fate. Hongjian cannot quite agree:

Hongjian launched into a discourse: "Take the group of people who are on the boat with us: we don't know a single one of them. We don't know why they're here and why they didn't take either an earlier or a later boat, so we consider the fact that we are all gathered together to be a coincidence. But if we were familiar with their situations and plans, then we would know that their taking this boat was no coincidence and that they had their reasons for taking this particular one, just as we did. It's like listening to the radio. If you turn the dial full circle, you'll hear this station with its phrase or two of Peking opera, a half sentence of an announcement from that station; suddenly there'll be a snatch of foreign music, a few words, a tune, a whole mish-mash all mixed together and incomprehensible. But on the program of the station it's coming from, each of these fragments has a context and isn't garbled at all. You just have to decide on a station to listen to and you'll understand its meaning. Our contacts with other people are just like this, strangers that we don't know well—" (294-95/307-308)

The monologue is interrupted when Roujia yawns at it. Its point, however, is clear on at least three levels. On the level that is interior to Hongjian's character, he becomes aware of the arbitrariness of human relations. It is simultaneously a real gain of knowledge about the difficulties through which he has been and a rationalization. To the extent that it is an increase in wisdom, we can see that, had he realized this and acted upon this realization earlier, he would not have indulged in the futile bouts of temper which caused him so much trouble. On the plot level, the episode illustrates the estrangement between Hongjian and Roujia that underscores the sequence to follow. A fight breaks out between him and Roujia when he sees her yawning, and he abruptly ceases his speech. The misunderstanding is the perfect representation of the truth he has just uttered: Roujia and Hongjian demonstrate that they are not on the same wave length, and his anger shows the degree to which his philosophizing is an attempt to paper over his discontent. Finally, on the meta-textual level, the discourse addresses itself to the arbitrariness of Hongjian the intentional narrator. The world that unfolded through him is thus but one of many that he could have intended; there is nothing very privileged about it. But once that world has started to develop, once a choice is made and the needle is set, it makes a sense of its own regardless of his disposition toward it. Hongjian and the omniscient narrator speak as one here, setting up a paradox about the text itself. They tell us simultaneously that events have no inevitability about them, but that once set in motion, they can proceed in no other way.

Adding to Hongjian's chagrin, Roujia had revealed to him just before the beginning of this momentous speech that she had had a much firmer hold on reality over the past few months than he had. The year before on the boat out, Hongjian and Xinmei had been engaged in a conversation about women, and the talk had, as a matter of course, turned toward the subject of Roujia. Xinmei had given voice to suspicions that he had about her designs on them, which Hongjian had doubted. At the end of the conversation, they had discovered Roujia to be standing not far off, and they had wondered how much, if any, she had overheard. The issue was long forgotten when Hongjian was reminded of it by the similarity of the two situations of being on a ship's deck at night. In reply to his sudden query, she admits to having overheard most of the conversation and to have increased her regard for Hongjian because of his defense of her. The irony of this confession is that it confirms Xinmei's original suspicions about her. The result for Hongjian is that in the course of his ever-increasing manipulation by circumstance and his progressive realization of the consequences of other people's designs on him, he comes to see Roujia as the closest and most tangible representative of all the forces in the world which are impinging upon him. His resistance, therefore, focuses upon her, and she becomes the target of his abuse.

The notion of Roujia as last resort, however, has broader implications. With modern schooling and coming from a nuclear as opposed to an extended family, she represents as well the transvaluation of social mores in modern urban China. Among her many new Western ideals, she has adopted the notion of romantic love as the ultimate bastion against a hostile world. Her objection, for instance, to Hongjian's long speech on coincidence was that it interrupted a pleasant talk they were having about themselves: " 'We were just talking about us, so why did you have to bring in everybody on the boat and, for that matter, all of humanity?' " (294/308). She becomes jealous of Xinmei's influence over Hongjian and is also consciously pleased that she is gradually pulling Hongjian away from his own family. As with other representations of the idea that love conquers all in modern Chinese fiction, it is shown not to work.[23]

Sequence Five: Shanghai Again

The shrinking of perspective to which Fang falls victim in the last chapter descends inevitably to his breakup with Roujia. The fights and resulting breaches become ever more serious. Since there exists no common ground of understanding on which to heal these rifts, most of the fights are ended by the *chedan* method.

As in the novel as a whole, however, the ability to ignore the present situation and turn to another without consideration of consequence—which is the essence of the *chedan* style—becomes ever more impossible as units of causality are completed. It is thus an ominous point in the relationship between the couple when Roujia announces during one of their fights that " 'If you make light of this [*chedan*], I just won't pay any attention to you" (317/335). The utterance has multiple significance. It puts a limit on the extent to which the worsening conflicts with Roujia can be extended at the same time that it signifies that the narrative itself—now moving along strictly on the basis of Hongjian's explosions of temper—is rapidly losing elasticity. But then neither Hongjian nor Roujia can summon up the resolve to take a principled stand toward their relationship; when the final fight comes, it is not the result of any sudden realization by either party but the tying together of a string of apparently insignificant and arbitrary events.

As events in the novel come to a head, the force of historical circumstance, so long merely a muted presence in the background, is suddenly thrust to the fore to take a clear and powerful place in the narrative. This intrusion, made by the omniscient narrator, begins innocently enough with an interior monologue in which Hongjian ponders the paradox of his feeling that Sanlü University was too small while Shanghai is too big—another form of the basic paradox of the besieged city:

Feelings of loneliness in a crowd and desolation amid bustle caused him, like so many others in this isolated island, to sense his own soul to be a scattered isolated island. There was an enormous change between the Shanghai of this year and last. The situation in Europe had steadily deteriorated, so Japan took advantage of this to run wild in the two foreign concessions. The England and America that were later to "fight shoulder to shoulder" with China were then only interested in preserving their neutral stance. But their neutrality wasn't really neutral and their stance was fundamentally unsteady. As a result, this "neutral stance" transformed itself into simply seeking some sort of toehold in China, and aside from this, everything was given to Japan to trample at will. John Bull uttered nothing but "bull" and Uncle Sam was revealed to be Uncle Sham. . . . The United States continued to send boatload after boatload of scrap iron to Japan, England was considering closing off the Burma road. . . . Commodity prices were like a kite with a broken string, or like a sage who had achieved immortality—they flew straight up into the air. . . . The struggle for existence was gradually being stripped of its ornamental mask and revealing its primitive savagery. Basic integrity could no longer be regarded as quite so basic. Those who took advantage of the national tragedy to grow rich and those who were ruined by the national tragedy both grew in number, but they had nothing to do with one another, since the poor could beg only on the public streets and were not able to go to the quiet courtyards of the rich. Slums spread like ringworm across the face of the city. Acts of political terrorism took place almost every day, and people of principle were forced, like the transportation systems of Western cities, to go underground. The vermin with human forms which had been underground gradually latched onto [men of principle] to increase their own reputations. Those newspapers which promoted "peace between China and Japan" every day published new lists of those who had joined their cause, but these traitors always simultaneously proclaimed their "non-involvement with politics" in other newspapers. (308–309/324–25)

Although this passage begins in Hongjian's mind, it is quickly taken over by the omniscient narrator. The most obvious signal of this is the phrase "The England and America that were later to . . . ," information plainly unavailable to Hongjian. The extent and intricacy of the word play, much of which simply cannot be forced into English, is, however, an equally clear indicator. It is this passage which sets the tone for the disintegration of Hongjian's world. It reveals the full extent of the objective unravelling of Shanghai society; the events in which Hongjian takes part are a concretization of the general truth.

Hongjian eventually secures a low-paying job at the newspaper. The immediate cause of the split between him and Roujia arises out of an insoluble disagreement between them about what he should do when the newspaper's management decides to knuckle under to Japanese pressure and change its editorial policy. Hongjian, in line with a prior agreement he has made with the editor, joins a mass resignation of the editorial staff without first gaining his wife's approval. When she finds out, she is angry, but then suggests that he go to work for her comprador aunt; summoning up his last vestige of propriety, Hongjian adamantly refuses. This sets the scene for the climactic and inevitable fight which ends the book. With the fight over and Roujia having gone to her aunt's residence, Hongjian returns to an empty house and falls asleep, a sleep which is described as being "without dreams, without sensations, which was at the same time a sample of death" (342/361).

Just before he falls into this sleep, however, he is said to have a sudden renewal of hope, an eventuality rendered supremely ironic by the description which follows his falling asleep: just then, the old clock which had been given him by his father begins to chime, but to chime a time five hours earlier, a time before the fight and the final dissolution of Hongjian's life. The clock has earlier been shown to be a symbol for Hongjian himself; Roujia has commented several times on their similarity of appearance. Its ringing out a time when there still was a tiny justification for the hopeful feeling which comes over him at the end—when all possible bases for such a feeling have vanished—makes a final vivid contrast between Hongjian's subjective feelings and the objective circumstances. This creates a double mirror effect, in which the chiming clock throws the reader back in an infinite loop from the time after the fight is long over back to the time before it began. It is as if Hongjian, being only capable of knowledge after the fact, is doomed forever to repeat his mistakes and not to reach harmony between his own consciousness and the external world. For this reason, the omniscient narrator, in a tone far grander than anything available to the pitiful Fang, closes the novel by describing the clock as "unintentionally embracing an irony and sadness toward life deeper than any language, or tears, or laughter" (342/361). With these words, the melancholy and hopeless mood frame which had begun the narrative is finally, along with the book itself, closed.

Chapter Seven
A Short Evaluation

The years immediately following 1945 when Qian Zhongshu published his three most famous volumes were unkind to all authors, but particularly to those of Qian's urbane bent. The publishing world was in disarray, and the wave of political determination which swept through the literary community drastically reduced commitment to literary values. To the extent that authors were still writing, they turned to revolution and to the depiction of workers and peasants. Qian's fiction did attract both critical attention and readers in those years, but most of the attention was given to more or less hostile expressions of disappointment that such obvious talent should have been devoted to such a trivial enterprise. And while his fiction sold relatively well, books on the contemporary political situation sold much better. The times were simply not propitious for fiction of manners, no matter how deeply it probed to the ultimate significance of those manners.

The academic side of Qian has become better known over the years. *Tan Yi Lu* has won increasing recognition as a uniquely rich and insightful commentary on Chinese poetry and poetics. *The Pipe-Awl Chapters* will no doubt fare as well as the four volumes become generally available. The scholar Qian in the years since 1977 has become something of a public institution, held up in both China and (albeit in a much smaller circle) the West as a model of both erudition and wit. The praise that accompanies such high stature, however, inevitably surrounds its object with a complaisance that even Qian's barbed humor cannot entirely dispel. The image being created of "leading man of letters" and cultural giant, no matter how true, runs the danger of submerging that side of him that would have gleefully and pointedly lampooned such adulation had it happened to someone else.

In trying to summarize the whole of Qian's career, the antinomies multiply rather than diminish. He is simultaneously scholar and satirist; *Tan Yi Lu,* a work in one of the most traditional scholarly forms, is informed at key points by Hegelian aesthetics; *Fortress Besieged* is a novel that could have been written by a slightly more earnest (or, when earnest, less maudlin) Evelyn Waugh, yet the Chinese used to compose it represents a sureness of style unmatched by any other May Fourth writer. Perhaps the last word is that Qian was aware of the odd juxtapositions of his life and writing, that he did not grow morose about his own or his country's cultural fate but sought instead to use all the materials that had become "close at hand"—from both the West and China—to build what he could. In the process he had often to be negative and he often teased. It is hard to resist the conclusion, for instance, that the similarities between Fang Hongjian and his creator deliberately defy that Chinese critical convention of treating fiction as allegory of personal suffering and desire. There is in Qian the sense of high playfulness that he seems to share with other modern Chinese humanists such as Y. R. Chao and Achilles Fang.

To my mind, then, *Fortress Besieged* stands as the work that most sharply captures Qian's many facets. The novel seems at once to offer a distant and scathing overview of contemporary society and an almost tragic sense of knowledge coming forever too late to be of any use. This tragic sense is, of course—as Qian maintained in 1979—of a universal human condition. It also, however, speaks poignantly of the predicament of the modern Chinese intellectual, that man who—acting on obsolete assumptions—thought himself in control of history while ending up its victim. The brusque and intolerant reception the work was accorded in 1947–48 lends ironic testimony to its value: if there were anything that would have profited the righteous engaged intellectuals of the 1940s, it was the cold moment of introspection that Fang Hongjian's fate should have provoked.

The need for positive action in China after 1945 makes *Fortress*'s hard fate understandable: most Chinese agreed then and would agree now that the bitter years after World War II were no time to laugh or even to engage in much self-searching. The headlong rush to political purity of those years, however, created problems still very evident today. Qian's satirical work anatomizes the root causes of some of those problems. The news of the novel's republication in late 1980 in Peking in a large printing gives favorable indication that *Fortress* is on its way to gaining the place in the ongoing tradition of Chinese letters that it has long deserved.

Notes and References

Preface

1. Xia Zhiqing [C. T. Hsia], "Cong Hui Qian Zhongshu Jishi" (Record of Meeting Qian Zhongshu Again), *Zhongguo Shibao,* (June 1979), pp. 16–17.

Chapter One

1. Leo Lee, *The Romantic Generation of Modern Chinese Writers* (Cambridge, Mass.: Harvard University Press, 1973), esp. chapter 12.
2. Interview with Qian Zhongshu, 11 May 1979.
3. Zhao Jingshen, *Wentan Yijiu* [Memories of the Literary Stage] (Shanghai: Beixin, 1948), p. 120.
4. Zou Wenhai, "Yi Qian Zhongshu" [Remembering Qian Zhongshu], *Zhuanji Wenxue* I.1 (June 1962):23–24.
5. See Chapter 3, pp. 47–48.
6. Qian Jibo, "Zi Zhuan" [Autobiography], *Guanghua Daxue Banyuekan* III.8 (1935). Reprinted as appendix to *Xiandai Zhongguo Wenxue Shi* [History of Contemporary Chinese Literature] (Hong Kong: Longmen, 1965). References will be to the Hong Kong edition.
7. Zou Wenhai, "Remembering Qian Zhongshu," p. 23.
8. C. T. Hsia, "Meeting Qian Zhongshu."
9. Qian Zhongshu, "Lin Shu de Fanyi" [The Translations of Lin Shu], in *Jiu Wen Sipian* [Four Old Essays] (Shanghai, 1979), p. 66.
10. Interview with Luo Xianglin, 26 February 1976.
11. Letter from Qian Zhongshu, dated 7 March 1937, in *T'ien Hsia Monthly* IV.4 (April 1937):427.
12. According to Zou Wenhai, "Remembering Qian Zhongshu," p. 23, Qian was undertaking such factual scholarship even in primary school.
13. Mai Bingkun, "Qian Zhongshu de Shengping he Zhushu" [Qian Zhongshu's Life and Works], *Ming Bao Yuekan* 128 (August 1976):51–52.
14. Qian Zhongshu, "The Translations of Lin Shu," p. 90.
15. Martin Green, *Children of the Sun* (New York: Basic Books, 1976), p. 72.

16. See Hubert Freyn, *Chinese Education in the War* (Shanghai: Kelly and Walsh, 1940), pp. 34–40.

17. Interview with Wang Zuoliang, 11 May 1980.

18. Qian Zhongshu, *Tan Yi Lu* [Discourses on Art] (Shanghai, 1948), p. i. Although this work is referred to by the slightly erroneously translated title *On the Art of Poetry* by C. T. Hsia, E. M. Gunn, and by the translators of *Fortress Besieged,* I shall use the title by which it is best known.

19. See Edward M. Gunn, *Unwelcome Muse* (New York, 1980), pp. 110–15.

20. Interview with Song Qi, 29 February 1976.

21. See T. D. Huters, "Critical Ground: The Transformation of the May Fourth Tradition," in Bonnie McDougall, ed., *Popular Literature and the Performing Arts in the People's Republic of China* (forthcoming).

22. The prefaces to *Tan Yi Lu, Humans, Beasts and Ghosts* and *Fortress Besieged* are dated respectively 15 July 1942, 1 April 1944, and 15 December 1946. *Tan Yi Lu* has, however, a supplementary note of 15 April 1948 indicating that a few additions had been made after 1942. The story "Linggan" [Inspiration] in *Humans, Beasts and Ghosts* refers to the atomic bomb, suggesting that at least some work was done on that story after August 1945. As *Fortress Besieged* began to be serialized in February 1946, the preface was probably written after the work was completed.

23. Huters, "Critical Ground."

24. Allyn and Adele Rickett, *Prisoners of Liberation* (Garden City, N.Y.: Doubleday Anchor, 1973), p. 39. Qian is given the pseudonym "Jao'" in this work.

25. Interview with Qian Zhongshu. See also Fang Dan, "Wo suo Renshi de Qian Zhongshu" [The Qian Zhongshu I Know], *Ming Bao Yuekan* 164 (August 1979):42–43.

Chapter Two

1. Zhao Jingshen, *Memories of the Literary Stage,* p. 120.

2. Qian Zhongshu, "[Review of] Zhongguo Xin Wenxue de Yuanliu," in "Shubao Chunqiu" [Publishing Annals], *Xin Yue Yuekan* IV.4 (November 1932):9. Pagination begins anew with each section of each number of this journal. Subsequent page references to this article will be inserted in the text at the end of each quotation.

3. The Chinese is *shi zhe chi ye,* quoted by Liu Xie (d. ca. 523) in *Wenxin Diaolong,* ch. 26 *(Wenxin Diaolong Zhu* [Taipei: Minglun,

1975], p. 65). The translation is by James J. Y. Liu, *Chinese Theories of Literature* (Chicago: University of Chicago Press, 1975), p. 126. Liu Xie is quoting from the *Shi Wei Han Shenwu* [Apocryphal Commentary on the Classic of Poetry].

4. This sentence, being based on the similarity in Chinese between "revolution" *(geming)* and "obedience" *(zunming)*, loses badly in translation.

5. "The revolution has not yet succeeded. . . . [A]ll my comrades must continue to exert their efforts . . ." is probably the most famous sentence from the "will" that Sun Yat-sen wrote some two weeks before he died in March 1925. See Lyon Sharman, *Sun Yat-sen* (Stanford: Stanford University Press, 1968), p. 308.

6. Qian Zhongshu, "[Review of] *Jindai Sanwen Chao*," in "Shubao Chunqiu," *Xin Yue Yuekan* VI.7 (June 1933):1–2. For discussion of Zhang Xuecheng's notion, see David Nivison, *The Life and Thought of Chang Hsueh-ch'eng* (Stanford: Stanford University Press, 1966), pp. 127–33.

7. Qian Zhongshu, "[Review of] *Luo Ri Song*," in "Shubao Chunqiu," *Xin Yue Yuekan* IV.6 (March 1933):21.

8. Ibid., pp. 26–27. The final sentence in this description is clearly, although unacknowledgedly, derived from the opening quatrain of William Blake's *Auguries of Innocence*, which reads, "To see a World in a Grain of Sand / And a Heaven in a Wild Flower / Hold Infinity in the palm of your hand / And Eternity in an hour." See Frank Kermode et al., eds., *Oxford Anthology of English Literature* (New York: Oxford University Press, 1973), II, 69.

9. C. S. Ch'ien [Qian Zhongshu], "Tragedy in Old Chinese Drama," *T'ien Hsia Monthly* I.1 (August 1935):37.

10. Actually, Babbitt accuses the Chinese of "failure to achieve a great ethical art like that of the drama and the epic of the Occident at their best." He speculates that to have achieved this ethical art, "the Confucians would have needed to work out a sound conception of the role of the imagination—the universal key to human nature—and this they do not seem to have done." (Irving Babbitt, *Rousseau and Romanticism* [New York: Meridian Books 1955], Appendix: "Chinese Primitivism," p. 299.) Looked at in its entirety, then, Babbitt's concept bears a certain resemblance to that of Qian as set forth in his review of *Odes to the Setting Sun*. Qian's notion of hierarchies of values does not contradict this; rather, it offers an explanation of the limitations placed on the development of a Confucian theory of the imagination.

11. Throughout this essay Qian's description of Western tragedy is heavily dependent upon A. C. Bradley. Cf. Bradley on the distinction between tragic and poetic justice:

The catastrophe is, in the main, the return of this [critical] action on the head of the agent. It is an example of justice; and that order which, present alike within the agents and outside them, infallibly brings it about, is therefore just. The rigour of its justice is terrible, no doubt, for a tragedy is a terrible story; but in spite of fear and pity, we acquiesce, because our sense of justice is satisfied.

Now, if this view is to hold good, the "justice" of which it speaks must be at once distinguished from what is called "poetic justice." "Poetic justice" means that prosperity and adversity are distributed in proportion to the merits of the agents. Such "poetic justice" is in flagrant contradiction with the facts of life, and it is absent from Shakespeare's tragic pictures of life.

A. C. Bradley, *Shakespearean Tragedy* (London: Macmillan 1965), pp. 22-23.

12. At about the same time, Osbert Sitwell in England developed the notion of "Chinese temperament," which included the idea that "subordination of man's will has prevented China from achieving a science." See Green, *Children of the Sun,* p. 264.

13. C. S. Ch'ien [Qian Zhongshu], "Foreword" to Cyril Drummond Le Gros Clark, *The Prose Poetry of Su Tung-p'o* (Shanghai, 1935), p. xiii.

14. Qian develops this idea at greater extent and complexity in *Tan Yi Lu*. For a discussion of it, see Chapter 3, pp. 40-41.

15. There was, for instance, an article by Qian announced for the fourth issue of Zhu Guangqian's *Wenxue Zazhi,* which was announced for August of 1937. If that issue ever appeared, it is very rare.

16. This balanced view of the knotty problem of "literary influence" tallies with F. O. Matthiessen's description of the attitudes of the writers of the "American Renaissance" toward the same issue: "Emerson knew that each age turns to particular authors of the past, not because of the authors but because of its own needs and preoccupations that those authors help make articulate. As Thoreau said, 'The researcher is more memorable than the researched.' " F. O. Matthiessen, *American Renaissance* (New York: Oxford University Press 1968), pp. 101-102.

Qian's article is entitled "Chinese Literature," and can be found in *The Chinese Year Book 1944-45* (Seventh Issue), ed. Cao Wenyan (Shanghai, 1945), ch. VIII. The passage cited is on p. 115. Succeeding page references to this article will appear in the text.

17. C. S. Ch'ien [Qian Zhongshu], "The Return of the Native," *Philobiblon* 4 (March 1947):10. The *locus classicus* for Confucius's statement is *Lun Yu*, IV.8. *Tan Yi Lu* contains a very similar discussion on pp. 280–81.

18. Qian Zhongshu, "Zhongguo Shi yu Zhongguo Hua" [Chinese Poetry and Chinese Painting] (Hong Kong, 1969), p. 1. This article was originally published in 1947 as part of a volume commemorating the twentieth anniversary of the Kaiming Book Company. It has recently been reprinted in Qian's 1979 collection, *Four Old Essays*.

19. Qian Zhongshu, *Song Shi Xuan Zhu* [Annotated Anthology of Song Poetry] (Peking, 1958). Qian has much to say in *Tan Yi Lu* about the conventional periodizing of Chinese literature; see my summary of his arguments in Chapter 3 below, pp. 40–45.

20. Qian develops a more sophisticated and problematic theory of the nature of historical writing in *Tan Yi Lu*. For discussion, see Chapter 3, pp. 47–48.

21. The difficulties of maintaining the tradition in the face of contemporary political tumult are indicated by the widely circulated story that the *Annotated Anthology* was withdrawn for ideological reasons soon after its 1958 publication. Qian denied this in my 1979 interview with him, asserting that the book's scarcity was due to a combination of a relatively small print run (15,000 copies) and its wide popularity as a college text.

22. Zhongguo Kexue Yuan Wenxue Yanjiusuo Zhongguo Wenxue Shi Bianxie Zu, ed., *Zhongguo Wenxue Shi* (Peking: Renmin Wenxue, 1962), Vol. II.

23. Qian Zhongshu, "Tonggan" [Synaesthesia], *Wenxue Pinglun* 1 (1962):13–17. This has also been republished in *Four Old Essays*.

24. Qian Zhongshu, "Du 'Laaokong' " [Reading *Laocoon*], *Wenxue Pinglun* 5 (1962):66. This article has also been included in *Four Old Essays*.

25. Qian Zhongshu, "Lin Shu de Fanyi" [The Translations of Lin Shu], in *Four Old Essays* (Shanghai, 1979), pp. 62–95. This article has been partially and rather freely translated by George Kao as "Lin Chinnan Revisited," in *Renditions* 5 (Autumn 1975):8–21.

26. The translator Arthur Waley shares that opinion. See "Arthur Waley on Lin Shu," *Renditions* 5 (Autumn 1975):30–31.

27. For the idea that Lin Shu made fiction "respectable," see Cheng Chen-to, "A Contemporary Appraisal of Lin Shu," *Renditions* 5 (Autumn 1975):26–29.

Chapter Three

1. Qian notes in the preface to *Tan Yi Lu* that ". . . in the confusion [of war], I had no books. While not yet old, I am forgetful and, although sober, make errors. I had no way to gain explanation for various uncertainties, as there were few means to check things." He does note, however, that he secured help by mail from various scholars. See *Tan Yi Lu* (Shanghai, 1948), pp. i–ii.

2. See C. T. Hsia, *History of Modern Chinese Fiction*, p. 433, and Helmut Martin, "A Transitional Concept of Chinese Literature 1897–1917," *Oriens Extremis* XX.2 (December 1973):200. C. T. Hsia, however, in his latest writings on Qian, has recanted of this opinion.

3. Ch'ien Chung-shu [Qian Zhongshu], "Classical Literary Scholarship in Modern China" (Peking, 1978), p. 2.

4. The Chinese is *fu ming bu chen*, which seems to be a variation on the line, *wo sheng bu chen*, from Ode #257, "Sang Rou," of the *Xiao Ya* in the *Classic of Poetry*. Karlgren translates the *Xiao Ya* line as "I was born (untimely) at an unhappy time." See Bernhard Karlgren, *The Book of Odes* (Stockholm: the Museum of Far Eastern Antiquities, 1974), p. 221.

5. This couplet is from Du Fu's poem "Si Song" [Four Pines], in the *Du Shi Yinde* [A Concordance to the Poems of Tu Fu] (Taipei: Ch'eng-wen, 1966), II, 144.19. It has been translated by Rewi Alley in *Tu Fu: Selected Poems* (Hong Kong: Commercial, 1962), pp. 127–28; I have revised Alley's translation a good deal. The poem as a whole relates the narrator's return to his home in difficult times and his comparison of his own evanescent life with that of the four pines; he had planted them some time previous and they had survived his absence.

6. Xu Zhenqing (1479–1511) was one of the "Seven Early Masters" of the Ming dynasty. Known primarily as a poet, he wrote a *Tan Yi Lu*, which survives as an appendix in one *juan* to his poetry collection, *Di Gong Ji*. According to Hok-lam Chan, Xu's *Tan Yi Lu*, "a treatise of poetic theory regarded as an important contribution to the field, was printed in 1520." See Hok-lam Chan, "Hsu Chen-ch'ing," in L. Carrington Goodrich and Chaoying Fang, eds., *Dictionary of Ming Biography* (New York: Columbia University Press, 1976), I, 569–70.

7. The phrase I have translated as "This is also to show the futility of these changed times" reads literally, "This is also to show [how I]

have been transformed into a crane and vainly return home." It refers to Ding Lingwei, who, after becoming an immortal, transformed himself into a crane to revisit his old home. Upon his arrival, a youth shot at him, causing him to express his grief in lyrical form: "Returning home from a thousand-year absence: / City and country as of old, the people all changed." The allusion to estrangement from one's native land is made more intense by the fact that Ding's home was in what is now Manchuria, the first area of China to have been occupied by the Japanese.

"Where is the raven to stop" is from Ode #192, "Zheng Yue," the whole sequence being translated by Karlgren as "Look at the Raven, it stops on whose house?" (*Odes*, 135). It is an image of inauspiciousness. The Chinese for "the cassia does not beckon" is *gui bu liu ren*. I have not been able to find the source.

8. "Ai Jiangnan" [Mourning for Jiangnan] is the title of a *fu* written by Yu Xin (513–581) in his old age, lamenting the disorder that had come to his native place.

9. *Tan Yi Lu*, p. 1. Hereafter, page references to *Tan Yi Lu* will be given in parentheses following the passage cited.

10. See Chapter 2 above, p. 23.

11. In the interview of 11 May 1979, Qian mentioned that his own style of literary Chinese was just a combination of the parallel and the ordinary styles.

12. Zhou Zuoren's *Origins* is one of the best examples. For further discussion of this point, see Chapter 4.

13. This recalls Nietzsche's idea of the proper function of the writer of history, which, in the words of Hayden White, "was to think dramatistically," or, as Nietzsche himself wrote, "to think one thing with another, and weave the elements into a single whole, with the presumption that the unity of plan must be put into objects if it is not already there." Quoted by Hayden White in "Interpretation in History," *New Literary History* IV.2 (Winter 1973):284.

14. The Chinese for "It must have been so," *xiang dangran er*, is the capping line in an anecdote in which Kong Rong (153–208) castigates Cao Cao (155–220) for allowing his son, Cao Pi (187–226), to take as concubine the wife of the ruler of a town the Caos' had just captured. Kong wrote to Cao saying, "When Wu Wang conquered Zhou, he presented Da Ji to Zhou Gong [Wu Wang's brother]." This is a direct contradiction of the historical account, which tells of Wu Wang having had Da Ji decapitated and her head put on a flagpole, signifying the Zhou's ruin had been her fault. Cao replied that he did not understand

and asked Kong what he was alluding to. Kong's reply was: "Judging by the present [occasion], it must have been so." See the *Hou Han Shu* [History of the Latter Han Dynasty] (Peking: Zhonghua, 1965), *juan* 70, pp. 2271–72.

The other phrase, *mo xu you,* is recorded in the "Yue Fei Zhuan" [Biography of Yue Fei] of the *Song Shi* [Song History]. Upon hearing that Yue Fei (1103–1141), had just been put in prison, Han Shizhong (1089–1151), one of Yue's fellow generals, demanded the reason of chief minister Qin Gui (1090–1155). Qin replied that Yue's son Yue Yun (1119–1141) and Zhang Xian had been plotting treason, adding that "Although the letter between Yue Yun and Zhang Xian is not clear, the eventuality [of the plot], if not certain, is likely to be so."

Later scholars, aware that the phrase *mo xu you* does not make sense as it is here glossed, have questioned the veracity of this quote. Xu Qianxue (1631–1711), in *Zizhi Tongjian Houbian* [Supplement to the Comprehensive Mirror for Aid in Government], and Bi Yuan (1730–1797). in *Xu Zizhi Tongjian* [The Continued Comprehensive Mirror for Aid in Government], both give the phrase as *bi xu you,* and Zhu Yizun (1629–1709) agrees. The late Qing scholar Yu Zhengxie (1775–1840) believes that the phrase was compounded by Han Shizhong via a deliberate conflation of Qin Gui's vacillation on the case between "was not so" *(mo)* and "perhaps it was so" *(xu you),* so as to create the absurd combination of *mo xu you;* this, of course, made Qin and Yue Fei's imprisonment appear the more unjust. Qian Zhongshu's use of this phrase as an example of historical distortion thus appears particularly apt. For the general context, see Hellmut Wilhelm, "From Myth to Myth: The Case of Yueh Fei's Biography," in A. F. Wright and D. C. Twitchett, eds., *Confucian Personalities* (Stanford: Stanford University Press, 1962), esp. p. 160.

15. The text for Confucius is *Lun Yu,* VI.16, which reads in full, translated by Arthur Waley, as follows: "The Master said, When natural substance prevails over ornamentation, you get the boredom of the rustic. When ornamentation prevails over natural substance, you get the pedantry of the scribe. Only when ornament and substance are duly blended do you get the true gentleman." Trans. Arthur Waley, *The Analects of Confucius* (New York: Vintage, 1938), p. 119. Qian's bending of the sense of this passage leaves him, in turn, open to the charge of distorting history.

16. Cf. Gu Jiegang's opposite (and more prevalent) assumption:

One who . . . regards all traditions that have come down to us in the lyrics, the novels, and the dramas, as so much frivolous and uncanonical narration, may, it is true, be motivated by a laudable desire to eliminate fictitious elements from history, but actually he is reversing the true order of history. One who has no illusions on this matter will be able to perceive the indisputable facts of history that lie imbedded in imaginative literature, and at the same time will not be deceived by those accounts that have been laboriously compiled by learned scholars.

From Arthur W. Hummel, trans., *The Autobiography of a Chinese Historian* (Taipei: Ch'eng-wen, 1972), p. 132.

17. Qian Zhongshu, "Chinese Poetry and Chinese Painting," p. 1.

18. See Chia-ying Yeh Chao, "The Ch'ang-chou School of *Ts'u* Criticism," in Adele Rickett, ed., *Chinese Approaches to Literature from Confucius to Liang Ch'i-ch'ao* (Princeton: Princeton University Press, 1978), pp. 151–88, for a critical discussion of the allegorical tendency in Chinese poetics.

19. *Tan Yi Lu,* p. 55. Qian cites the passage as "The [*Li*] Sao contains resentment and criticism; its words touch on matters of governance and chaos. [Li] He does not have this." A more accepted version has the last line as a more ambiguous "probably doesn't have this." See Du Mu, "Li Changji Geshi Xu" [Preface to Li Changji's Poetry], in Wang Qi, ed., *Li Changji Geshi Huijie* [Collected Commentaries on Li Changji's Poetry], in *Sanjia Pingzhu Li Changji Geshi* [The Three Annotated Commentaries on Li Changji's Poetry] (Peking: Zhonghua, 1959), pp. 12–14.

20. See, for instance, Zhou Chengzhen, *Li He Lun* [On Li He] (Hong Kong: Wenyi, 1971), which has numerous unfavorable remarks on Qian's comments on Li He.

21. This poem is to be found on pp. 53–54 of *The Three Annotated Commentaries* edition. For a complete English translation, see J. D. Frodsham, *The Poems of Li Ho* (Oxford: Oxford University Press, 1970), p. 45.

22. Zhou Chengzhen in *On Li He,* p. 145, strenuously objects to Qian's characterization of this image on the grounds that it is now and was in the Tang common knowledge that clouds and water were ultimately the same substance.

23. For this poem, see *The Three Annotated Commentaries,* p. 56, and Frodsham, *Li Ho,* p. 56. Qian makes a similar point (with examples from other poets) about the extension of a comparison between two things beyond their shared attributes on p. 27 of *Tan Yi Lu.* He

Notes and References

compares the technique to the "conceits" of the English Metaphysical poets. Frodsham makes the point that such images both have an "inner logic" and "border on the synaesthesia of the Symbolists, whom Ho so much resembles." (p. xliii)

24. Zhou Chengzhen, *On Li He*, p. 148, in fact accuses Qian—rather than Li—of myopia.

25. See Chapter 4 for further discussion of this point.

26. For "Li Ping at the Harp," see *The Three Annotated Commentaries*, p. 35, and Frodsham, p. 10. For "Su Xiaoxiao's Tomb," see *The Three Annotated Commentaries*, p. 46, and Frodsham, p. 30.

27. The *locus classicus* is *Lun Yu*, VI.23.

28. For a recent statement of the view of Confucius as one divorced from considerations of aesthetics, see Donald Holzman, "Confucius and Ancient Chinese Literary Theory," in Rickett, ed., *Chinese Approaches to Literature*, pp. 21–41.

29. This poem is in *The Three Annotated Commentaries*, p. 148, and Frodsham, p. 206.

30. Li Bo, "Ri Chu Xing" [Ballad of the Rising Sun], in *Quan Tang Shi* [Complete Tang Poems] (Taipei: Minglun, 1971), *juan* 162, pp. 1687–88. Lu Yang is the subject of a story in the *Huai Nanzi* in which he, engaged in fierce battle as dusk approaches, brandishes his spear and forces the sun back.

31. This poem is in *The Three Annotated Commentaries*, pp. 138–39, and Frodsham, p. 190. The sunflower is an emblem of loyalty. Yi is the mythical archer who shot down nine of the ten suns which produced the intense heat referred to in the poem.

32. *Han Shu* [History of the Former Han Dynasty] (Peking: Zhonghua, 1964), *juan* 22, pp. 1059–60.

33. The translation is from James J. Y. Liu, *The Poetry of Li Shangyin* (Chicago: University of Chicago Press, 1969), p. 120. The original is to be found in *Complete Tang Poems*, *juan* 540, p. 6188.

34. Jiang Yan, "Hen Fu," in [Xiao Tong, Prince] Zhaoming [of Liang (501–531)], ed., *Wen Xuan* [Literary Anthology] (Taipei: Wenhua, 1955), *juan* 16, 16b.

35. These letters are in Han Yu, *Han Changli Wenji Jiaozhu* [Annotated Collection of Han Changli's Prose], pp. 389–91, included in *Han Changli Ji* [Collected Works of Han Changli] (Taipei: Heluo, 1975).

36. For a discussion of Han Yu and archaism, see Stephen Owen, *The Poetry of Meng Chiao and Han Yu* (New Haven: Yale University Press, 1975), pp. 8–23.

37. For more discussion on this point, see James J. Y. Liu, *Theories*, pp. 136–37.

38. See also Richard J. Lynn, "Orthodoxy and Enlightenment: Wang Shih-chen's Theory of Poetry and its Antecedents," in W. T. deBary, ed., *The Unfolding of Neo-Confucianism* (New York: Columbia University Press, 1975), pp. 217–69.

39. *Tan Yi Lu*, p. 241. The original can be found in Yuan Mei, *Suiyuan Shihua Buyi* [Supplement to Suiyuan Shihua] (Peking: Renmin Wenxue, 1960), I.1, p. 565. Qian's quotation differs somewhat from the original.

40. Yuan Mei, *Suiyuan Shihua* (Peking; Renmin Wenxue, 1960), VII.85, p. 241.

41. Ibid., III.66, p. 94.

42. The former poem is entitled "Xiari Guo Qinglongsi Ye Cao Chanshi" [On a Summer Day Visiting Qinglong Monastery to Call on Chang Master Cao] and can be found in *Complete Tang Poems, juan* 126, p. 1275. "Zhongnan Bieye" [Zhongnan Retreat] is in *juan* 126, p. 1276.

43. Aristotle, *Poetics*, trans. Ingram Bywater (New York: Modern Library 1954), IX, 235.

44. Geoffrey Hartman, "Crossing Over: Literary Commentary as Literature," *Comparative Literature* XXVIII.3 (Summer 1976):264.

45. C. S. Ch'ien [Qian Zhongshu], "Foreword," p. xiv.

46. Hartman, "Crossing Over," p. 264. The succeeding page reference to this article is given in the text.

47. Northrop Frye, *Anatomy of Criticism* (Princeton: Princeton University Press, 1957), pp. 341–42.

Chapter Four

1. Hu Shi, "Jianshe de Wenxue Geming Lun" [For a Constructive Literary Revolution], *Zhongguo Xin Wenxue Da Xi* [Comprehensive Anthology of the New Chinese Literature] (Hong Kong: Wenxue Yanjiu, 1962), I,155–56.

2. Zhou Zuoren, *Origins*, pp. 118–19. See also Achilles Fang, "Some Reflections on the Difficulty of Translation," in Arthur Wright, ed., *Studies in Chinese Thought* (Chicago: University of Chicago Press, 1953), p. 273.

3. Lu Xun, "Wo Zemma Xieqi Xiaoshuo Lai" [How I Came to Write Stories], *Nanqiang Beidiao Ji* [Mixed Dialects], p. 100 in *Lu Xun Sanshi Nian Ji* [Lu Xun: The Thirty Year Collection], VI. My translation differs

somewhat from that of Gladys and Hsien-yi Yang in *Selected Works of Lu Hsun* (Peking: Foreign Languages Press, 1964), III, 230.

4. For a summary of Gongan principles, see David Pollard, *A Chinese Look at Literature* (Berkeley: University of California Press, 1973), pp. 158–66.

5. Zhou Zuoren, *Origins,* p. 51; translated in Pollard, *Chinese Look,* p. 162.

6. Zhou Zuoren, "Daoyan" [Introduction] to *Comprehensive Anthology,* VI, 12.

7. See, for instance, the criticism of the Communist party leader Qu Qiubai in "The Question of Popular Literature and Art," trans. Paul Pickowicz, in J. Berninghausen and T. Huters, eds., *Revolutionary Literature in China* (White Plains, N.Y.: M.E. Sharpe, 1976), pp. 47–48.

8. Michel de Montaigne, "A Consideration upon Cicero," in *The Complete Essays of Montaigne,* I, 30, trans. Donald M. Frame (Stanford: Stanford University Press, 1958), pp. 184–85.

9. Rosalie Colie, "Burton's *Anatomy of Melancholy* and the Structure of Paradox," in Stanley Fish, ed., *Seventeenth Century Prose* (New York: Oxford University Press, 1971), p. 391.

10. Quoted in Morris Croll, "The Baroque Style in Prose," in Fish, ed., *Seventeenth Century Prose,* p. 48.

11. For an excellent exposition of the idea of writing as moral exercise, see Lynn, "Orthodoxy and Enlightenment," esp. pp. 217–21.

12. Lu Xun, "Kong Yiji," in *Na Han* [Call to Arms], p. 30, in *The Thirty Year Collection,* II. Translated by Gladys and Hsien-yi Yang in *Selected Works,* I, p.24.

13. Lu Xun, "Lun 'Feie Polai' Yinggai Huanxing" [On Deferring "Fair Play"], trans. Gladys Yang, in *Silent China* (London: Oxford University Press, 1973), p. 161. The Chinese text is in *Fen* [Graves], p. 255, *The Thirty Year Collection,* I. The translation has been slightly modified to replace specific allusions that Yang dropped.

14. Stanley E. Fish, *Self-Consuming Artifacts* (Berkeley: University of California Press, 1972), p. 86.

15. One of the most thoughtful and complete discussions of this need for a new critical attitude to replace the old habits of "stock response" is contained in Wu Shichang's article "Lun Cunchu Fanying" [On Stock Response], in *Zhongguo Wenhua yu Xiandaihua Wenti* [Chinese Culture and the Question of Modernization] (Shanghai: Guancha, 1948), pp. 81–89.

The idea of "stock response" was originally developed by I. A. Richards in his *Principles of Literary Criticism* (New York: Harcourt, Brace, 1925), pp. 202, 203. He explains its genesis and consequence as follows:

[A]s general reflection develops [from childhood on] the place of the free direct play of experience is taken by the deliberate organisation of attitudes, a clumsy and crude substitute. . . . Now reflection, unless very prolonged and very arduous, tends to fix the attitude[s] by making us dwell in [them], by *removing us from experience.* In the development of any attitude there are stages, points of rest, of relatively greater stability. These, as we dwell in them, become more and more difficult to pass. . . .

The losses incurred by these artificial fixations of attitudes are evident. Through them the average adult is worse, not better adjusted to the possibilities of his existence than the child. He is even in the most important things functionally unable to face facts: do what he will he is only able to face functions, fictions, projected by his own stock responses. Against these stock responses the artist's internal and external conflicts are fought, and with them the popular writer's triumphs are made. (Emphasis in original.)

16. Liu Xiwei [Li Jianwu], "Hua Meng Lu" [Record of Painted Dreams], in *Ju Hua Ji* [Tasting Flowers] (Shanghai: Wenhua Shenghuo, 1936), pp. 191–92.

17. Qian Zhongshu, "Discussing Friendship," *Wenxue Zazhi* I.1 (May 1937):187. Subsequent references to this essay will be given in the text after the passage cited.

18. Croll, "The Baroque Style," in Fish, ed., *Seventeenth Century*, p. 31. Croll uses the term "period" as synonymous with sentence. The analysis applies equally well to Qian's paragraphs.

19. Fish, *Self-Consuming Artifacts*, p. 83.

20. Croll, "The Baroque Style," in Fish, ed., *Seventeenth Century*, pp. 28–29.

21. The *locus classicus* is *Lun Yu*, XVI.4.

22. Qian Zhongshu, *Written on the Margin of Life* (Hong Kong, n.d.), p. i. All subsequent page references to this work will be given in the text.

23. "Yige Pianjian" [A Prejudice], pp. 48–53, has a similar faulty conjunction. The essay begins, "Prejudice can be said to be thought on vacation. It is the daily employ of the thoughtless but the Sunday amusement of the thoughtful." After dilating for a few sentences on the inevitability of a certain amount of mental laxity, Qian suddenly writes, "Of course, so-called truth and morality are at root nothing but prejudices." Syntactically, "Of course" implies a positive connection

with what has preceded it, but here it is working directly against the force of the earlier affirmation.

24. Wolfgang Iser, *The Implied Reader* (Baltimore: the Johns Hopkins University Press, 1974), p. 285.

25. This sort of opening is typical of the essays in the second half of the collection. "Du Yisuo Yuyan" [Reading *Aesop's Fables*], for instance, does not even mention the fables until halfway through its second page. "A Prejudice" does not tell what the prejudice is until fully halfway through the piece. The eighth essay, "Shi Wenmang" [Explaining Illiteracy], does not give us Qian's revised definition of "illiteracy" until the second page of the essay.

26. There is an even more explicit reference in the first essay, "Chuang" [Windows], when, in discussing the difference between doors and windows, Qian adds, "This, of course, is a distinction that applies only under normal social conditions; in abnormal situations such as war, the house itself cannot be guaranteed, so how can there be talk of doors and windows!" (13).

27. Richard Ohmann, "Modes of Order," in Donald C. Freeman, ed., *Linguistics and Literary Style* (New York: Holt, Rinehart and Winston, 1970), p. 223.

28. This method is most clearly employed in "Lun Kuaile" [On Happiness], in which—the case having been built for the wisdom of the person who realizes that happiness is determined subjectively—Qian ends by saying, "One who can preserve this attitude consistently is, of course, a great philosopher; but who can say that he is not also a great fool? Yes, this is a bit contradictory. Contradiction is the price paid for intelligence. This is the joke that life plays on philosophies of life" (22).

Charles J. Alber, in his excellent essay *"Wild Grass,* Symmetry and Parallelism in Lu Xun's Prose Poems," has pointed out a similar lack of resolution of parallel construction in Lu Xun's work. Alber's essay is to be found in William H. Nienhauser, ed., *Critical Essays on Chinese Literature* (Hong Kong: The Chinese University of Hong Kong, 1976), pp. 1–29. See esp. pp. 3–4.

29. C. S. Ch'ien [Qian Zhongshu], "The Return of the Native." p. 17.

Chapter Five

1. Qian Zhongshu, *Written on the Margin,* p. 3.

2. For elucidation of certain of such rules, see Mary Pratt, *Toward a Speech Act Theory of Literary Discourse* (Bloomington: University of

Indiana Press, 1977), pp. 101–16. One of the rules, for instance, is that "in conversation, one anecdote tends to follow another, and a single speaker rarely gets to tell two in succession" (108).

3. Gerard Genette, in "Boundaries of Narrative," *New Literary History* VIII.1 (Autumn 1976), makes much of the distinction between representation and dialogue and in fact puts the two forms on radically different levels in the narrative process. He holds that representation is a more intricate process than dialogue, having a more significant impact on the work in which they are contained. As he says:

One type of imitation [i.e., dialogue] is in direct relation while the other type [i.e., representation] calls for the intervention of a complex system of mediation. While we can admit with some difficulty that the operations of conceiving acts and conceiving words do proceed from a similar mental operation, "to say" these acts and "to say" these words constitute two very different verbal operations. More precisely, only the first act constitutes a real operation, that is, an act of diction in the Platonic sense, which requires a set of transpositions and equivalences as well as a set of unavoidable choices between those elements of a story to be retained and those to be omitted, choices between different possible points of view, etc. All of these operations are obviously absent when the poet or historian limits himself to transcribing a discourse. (4)

Qian's unique ability to depict conversation is at least partly a function of his having written during the war—it was only then, according to Sima Changfeng, that the vernacular language "matured. Because of the mass migrations of Chinese from various provinces, the dialects of each region were rationalized; this produced a rich new national language which can be called the 'national language of the war of resistance.' " Sima Changfeng, *Zhongguo Xin Wenxue Shi* [History of the New Chinese Literature] (Hong Kong: Zhaoming, 1976), II, 156.

4. Qian Zhongshu, *Written on the Margin*, p. 8.

5. Qian Zhongshu, *Humans, Beasts and Ghosts* (Hong Kong, n.d.), p. 1. All subsequent page references to this text will be given in parentheses after the passages cited.

6. William Lyell develops the concept of narrative "envelope" in his discussion of Lu Xun's style; it accords completely with what I shall call "frame." He defines "envelope" as "a special instance of repetition in which the repeated elements serve as the opening and final curtains of the entire story or of scenes within it." William A. Lyell, *Lu Hsün's*

Vision of Reality (Berkeley: University of California Press, 1976), p. 263.

7. C. T. Hsia, *History of Modern Chinese Fiction*, p. 434; pp. 434–36 give a plot summary of this story.

8. Robert Scholes and Robert Kellogg, *The Nature of Narrative* (New York: Oxford University Press, 1966), pp. 111–13.

9. Dorrit Cohn, "Narrated Monologue: Definition of a Fictional Style," *Comparative Literature* XVIII.2 (Spring 1966): 97. The two page references following are to this article.

10. The relative merits of the *Jing Pai* as opposed to the "Shanghai Clique" *(Hai Pai)* were a topic of debate in the early thirties. Lu Xun ridiculed it in his celebrated 1934 *zawen*, "Jing Pai yu Hai Pai," in *Huabian Wenxue* [Fringed Literature], pp. 21–22, in *The Thirty Year Collection*, vol. VII. Similarly, the literary salon came in for a good deal of abuse as being radically out of harmony with the hard times. The poet Feng Zhi wrote a particularly vigorous denunciation which ended with the words, "if we see in the newspaper the news of a salon-type evening gathering or discussion, and if these meetings are presided over by some banker or great lady or cultural expert, all it does is to make us feel a bit nauseated." See his "Shalong" [Salon], *Guancha* I.20 (16 November 1946):13.

11. See Wayne C. Booth, *The Rhetoric of Fiction* (Chicago: University of Chicago Press, 1961), pp. 169–209, for a discussion of the various ramifications of this term.

12. Qian Zhongshu, *Humans, Beasts and Ghosts*, p. i. C. T. Hsia, with characteristic perspicuity, comments that this disclaimer will have the consequence that "Even the most unwary reader, naturally, will be intrigued by this preface to guess the real identity of many a character in the book" *History of Modern Chinese Fiction*, p. 437.

13. Kai-yu Hsu, *The Chinese Literary Scene* (New York: Vintage, 1975), p. 18.

14. Jonathan Spence, in his review of *Fortress Besieged* ("Forever Jade," *New York Review of Books* XXVII.6 [17 April 1980]:20), suggests that the French ship name *Vicomte de Bragelonne* appearing on the first page of the novel may allude to the Alexandre Dumas *père* novel, *Dix Ans Plus Tard ou le Vicomte de Bragelonne,* and that the "ten years after" refers to the time between *Fortress*'s 1937 and the 1927 Shanghai massacre. Although I am generally skeptical of what seem to me to be Spence's overinterpretations, the contrast in both "The Cat" and *Fortress* between the palmy days of 1936–37 and the war years that followed would imply that the "ten years after" (if Qian was in fact alluding to it) refers

to the drastic contrast between the prewar years and the hard years around the end of the war when *Fortress* was being written and published. Cosmopolitan intellectuals of Qian's sort were much less moved by the events of 1927 than by the dismantling of their social position during the war against Japan.

Chapter Six

1. Qian Zhongshu, *Wei Cheng* [Fortress Besieged] (Shanghai, 1949), p. i.
2. Interview with Qian Zhongshu, 11 May 1979.
3. Ch'ien Chung-shu [Qian Zhongshu], "China in the English Literature of the Seventeenth Century," *Quarterly Bulletin of Chinese Bibliography* I.4 (December 1940):351.
4. A sequence is defined by Barthes as a "logical string of nuclei, linked together by a solidarity relation: the sequence opens when one of its terms is lacking an antecedent of the same kind, and it closes when another of its terms no longer entails any consequent function." Sequences do not, however, necessarily control the entire narrative within their bounds. Barthes notes that "before a sequence is completed, the initial terms of a fresh sequence can be introduced." Roland Barthes, "An Introduction to the Structural Analysis of Narrative," *New Literary History* VI.2 (Winter 1975):253, 255.

Qian's sequences are generally marked off by frames.

5. This episode bears an eerie resemblance to one in Kingsley Amis's *Lucky Jim*. Since the writing of *Fortress Besieged* preceded that of *Lucky Jim* by almost a decade and Amis presumably knows no Chinese, it is safe to rule out plagiarism. The similarity testifies to the general affinity Qian had for modern English life and letters, discussed in Chapter 1.
6. The novel in fact gets its name from a French proverb which runs: "Le mariage est comme une forteresse assiégée; ceux qui sont dehors veulent y entrer et ceux qui sont dedans veulent en sortir." This is quoted in the entry for *Wei Cheng* in the "Selected List of Chinese Publications" section of *Philobiblon* II.1 (January–June 1947):44. Qian being the editor of this journal, it is probable that he wrote the entry himself. Other information supplied about the novel in the space is that it is "a novel about the Chinese intelligentsia in wartime" and that it is a "bestseller."
7. Russian formalist critics cited this

"Architectonic totality," the recurrence of the same episode in a novel, a ballad, or a folk song [as serving] . . . the same esthetic purpose as "verbal tautology"—alliteration, refrain, rhythmical parallelism. In either case what could have been a straightforward statement is twisted by artful detours into a bizarre, multi-storied edifice.

See Victor Erlich, *Russian Formalism* (The Hague: Mouton 1969), p. 243.

8. Zbigniew Slupski, for instance, in writing about Lao She, notes the unevenness of tone which harms that writer's first two novels, *Lao Zhang de Zhexue* [The Philosophy of Zhang] and *Zhao Ziyue*. See *The Evolution of a Modern Chinese Writer* (Prague: N.P., 1966), p. 50. This problem of narrative tone was also present in Qian's earlier story, "God's Dream."

9. See, for instance, Tang Shi's review of Shi Tuo's *Marriage*, in which, although listing *Fortress* as one of modern China's two best novels (the other being Mao Dun's *Ziye* [Midnight]), he faults Qian for his overly intrusive voice in the text, which results in a work that is ultimately "a sheet of loose sand, with a desultory ending." See *Wen Xun* VIII.3 (March 1948):473. A reviewer in the Shanghai *Da Gong Bao* "Shu Ping" [Book Review] section voices a similar, if somewhat harsher, opinion. He maintains that Qian pays attention to plot only as a vehicle for exhibiting the brilliance of his writing style. See Bing Xi, "*Wei Cheng* Du Hou" [Having Read *Fortress Besieged*], *Da Gong Bao*, 19 August 1947.

10. Booth, *The Rhetoric of Fiction*, p. 332.

11. One critic in fact chastises Qian for taking just such an Olympian view of reality and thereby making it impossible for the reader to develop any sympathy for the characters. See Wu Jiu, "Du *Wei Cheng*" [Reading *Fortress Besieged*], *Xiaoshuo Yuekan* I.1 (July 1948):90–91.

12. Qian Zhongshu, *Wei Cheng*, pp. 1–2; Jeanne Kelly and Nathan Mao, trans., *Fortress Besieged* (Bloomington: University of Indiana Press, 1979). All further page references to these works will be cited in the text following the quotation. The first reference will be to the Chinese edition of 1948 and the second, in italics, will be to the translation. All translations are my own.

13. Thomas Hardy, *The Mayor of Casterbridge* (New York: Random House, 1950), pp. 17–18.

14. See James J. Y. Liu, *Theories*, pp. 17–18.

15. Cf. the review of Wu Jiu, "Reading *Fortress Besieged*," in which the section criticizing Qian's view of character and reality is entitled "Shangdi de Meng" [God's Dream].

16. Matthiessen, *American Renaissance*, p. 284.

17. For a discussion of this narrative method, see Booth, *Rhetoric of Fiction,* p. 153.

18. *Ganma* is the term for a sort of nonreligious "godmother"; *gannüer* is the daughter in such a relationship. In their translation, Kelly and Mao conveniently put all of Fang's interior monologue in italics.

19. Herman Melville, *The Confidence Man* (New York and Indianapolis: Bobbs-Merrill, 1967), p. 45.

20. Scholes and Kellogg, *Nature of Narrative,* p. 112.

21. The Russian formalist Viktor Sklovskij developed the theory of parallel characters which illuminate each other; see Victor Erlich, *Russian Formalism,* pp. 244–45.

22. This is a very old motif in Chinese literature. See, for example, David Hawkes's explanation of its employment in the *Chu Ci:*

The idea of the *progress,* the ritual journey—usually a ritual circuit—made for the purpose of affirming or acquiring, or both affirming and acquiring, power appears in Chinese tradition in many contexts and at many levels. It is essentially magical; but its travel may be real or imaginary, and the traveler may be a wizard, a mystic, or a king. It postulates a symmetrical cosmos whose various parts are presided over by various powers. These powers can be induced to give either their submission or their support to the traveler who approaches them with the correct ritual. A complete and successful circuit of the whole cosmos will therefore make him a lord of the universe, able to command any of its powers at will, if he is a wizard; to move in it with utter freedom, if he is a mystic; to rule by divine right and title with the allegiance of both temporal and spiritual powers, if he is an emperor.

See "The Quest of the Goddess," in Cyril Birch, ed., *Studies in Chinese Literary Genres* (Berkeley: University of California Press, 1974), p. 54.

The irony attached to Fang's new wisdom is apparent.

23. Some examples include Lu Xun's "Shang Shi," translated by Gladys and Hsien-yi Yang as "Regret for the Past," Mao Dun's treatment of the Zhang Manqing-Zhu Jinru subplot in his novella *Zhuiqiu* [Pursuit] and even Ba Jin's novel *Cold Nights.*

Selected Bibliography

I have not seen those works marked with an asterisk.

PRIMARY SOURCES

1. Works Published in One Volume (in chronological order)

Xie zai Rensheng Bianshang [Written on the Margin of Life]. *Shanghai, 1941(?); Hong Kong: Yixin, n.d.

Ren, Shou, Gui [Humans, Beasts and Ghosts]. Shanghai: Kaiming, 1946; Hong Kong: Yixin, n.d. A note attached to the table of contents of this volume announces that the story "Linggan" [Inspiration] was first published in the Shanghai magazine *Xin Yu*, I.2, and that "Mao" [The Cat] first appeared in *Wenyi Fuxing*, I.1.

Wei Cheng [Fortress Besieged]. Shanghai: Chenguang, 1947; *1948; 1949; Hong Kong: Jiben, 1969; Peking: Renmin Wenxue, 1980. *Wei Cheng* was first published serially in *Wenyi Fuxing*, I.2 to II.3, which appeared between February 1946 and January 1947. The first edition in book form was issued in May 1947 in 479 pages; it is clear and has few typographical errors. The third edition (and probably the second) was reset in a tighter format at 342 pages; it is poorly produced and has many typos. Unfortunately, the first edition is rare, and the various Hong Kong reprints are of the third edition, so my page references are to this readily available text.

Tan Yi Lu [Discourses on Art]. Shanghai: Kaiming, 1948; Hong Kong: Longmen, 1965. The work is also reprinted in Taiwan from time to time (generally rather sloppily), depending upon the vagaries of the political climate there.

Song Shi Xuan Zhu [Annotated Anthology of Song Poetry]. Peking: Renmin Wenxue, 1958; Peking: Renmin Wenxue, 1979. The poems in the two editions are almost identical (six from the 1958 edition have been deleted and one added to the 1979 version);

some material has been added to the 1979 annotations. Ten biographies from this work were first published in *Wenxue Yanjiu,* 1957.1. The "Introduction" first appeared in *Wenxue Yanjiu,* 1957.3.

Jiu Wen Sipian [Four Old Essays]. Shanghai: Guji, 1979. This book includes "Zhongguo Shi yu Zhongguo Hua," "Du 'Laaokong,' " "Tonggan," and "Lin Shu de Fanyi."

*Guanzhui Pian [Pipe-Awl Chapters]. Peking: Zhonghua, 1979–80. 4 vols.

Qian Zhongshu Xuanji [Selected Works of Qian Zhongshu]. Hong Kong: Wenxue Yanjiu, n.d. A collection of Qian's short pieces, including the contents of *Ren, Shou, Gui, Xie zai Rensheng Bianshang,* and "Zhongguo Shi yu Zhongguo Hua," with a short introduction.

2. Other Works (by date of publication).

Zhongshu Jun [Qian Zhongshu]. "Xiaoshuo Suozheng" [Sundry Inquiries on Fiction]. *Qinghua Zhoukan* 34.4 (22 November 1930):7–9. Pursuit of factual matters.

Zhongshu Jun. "[Review of] *Zhongguo Xin Wenxue de Yuanliu* [by Zhou Zuoren]." In "Shubao Chunqiu." *Xin Yue Yuekan* IV.4 (November 1932):9–15.

Zhongshu Jun. "[Review of] *Physiology of Beauty* [by Arthur Sewell]." In "Shubao Chunqiu." *Xin Yue Yuekan* IV.5 (December 1932):1–8.

Zhongshu Jun. "[Review of] *Luori Song* [by Cao Baohua]." In "Shubao Chunqiu." *Xin Yue Yuekan* IV.6 (March 1933):19–28.

Zhongshu Jun. "[Review of] *Jindai Sanwen Chao* [edited by Shen Qiwu]." In "Shubao Chunqiu." *Xin Yue Yuekan* IV.7 (June 1933):1–4.

Ch'ien Chung-shu. "Epilogue." *Guoli Qinghua Daxue Niankan* [National Qinghua University Yearbook]. Peking, n.p., 1933. An English essay appended to the college yearbook of which he was "English editor."

*"Zhongguo Wenxue Xiaoshi Xulun" [Prolegomena to a Short History of Chinese Literature]. *Guofeng Banyuekan* III.8 (1933). An article of about eight thousand characters. The *Short History* itself was apparently never published. According to Mai Bingkun, Qian published about one hundred Song-style poems in *Guofeng Banyuekan* between 1933 and 1935.

"Lun Buge" [On Lack of Obstruction]. *Xuewen Yuekan* I.3 (July 1934):76–81. Discusses translation theory and applies Wang

Guowei's idea of a "lack of obstruction" to the literary presentation of an image, rather than to the nature of the image itself.

C. S. Ch'ien. "Tragedy in Old Chinese Drama." *T'ien Hsia Monthly* I.1 (August 1935):37–46. Reprinted in *Renditions*, No. 9 (Spring 1978):85–91.

C. S. Ch'ien. "Foreword" to Cyril Drummond Le Gros Clark, trans. *The Prose Poetry of Su Tung-p'o*. Shanghai: Kelly and Walsh, 1935, pp. xiii–xxii. This piece was published in Chinese translation in *Xuewen Yuekan* I.2 (1934).

C. S. Ch'ien. "Correspondence." *T'ien Hsia Monthly* IV.4 (April 1937):425–27.

"Tan Jiaoyou" [Discussing Friendship]. *Wenxue Zazhi* I.1 (May 1937):187–97.

*"Zhongguo Guyou de Wenxue Piping de Yige Tedian" [A Characteristic of China's Own Literary Criticism]. *Wenxue Zazhi* I.4 (August 1937). Although announced, I do not know whether or not this issue of the journal ever appeared.

Ch'ien Chung-shu. "China in the English Literature of the Seventeenth Century." *Quarterly Bulletin of Chinese Bibliography* I.4 (December 1940):351–84.

Ch'ien Chung-shu. "China in the English Literature of the Eighteenth Century: I." *Quarterly Bulletin of Chinese Bibliography* II.1–2 (1941):7–48.

Ch'ien Chung-shu. "China in the English Literature of the Eighteenth Century: II." *Quarterly Bulletin of Chinese Bibliography* II.3–4 (December 1941):113–52.

Ch'ien Chung-shu, "Chinese Literature." In *The Chinese Year Book 1944–45* (seventh issue). Edited by Cao Wenyan. Shanghai: Shanghai Daily Tribune, 1945, pp. 115–28.

"Tan Zhongguo Shi" [Discussing Chinese Poetry]. *Da Gong Bao*, 14 December 1945. The Chinese translation of a condensed version of a speech given at the United States Army Officers Club on 6 December 1945.

C. S. Ch'ien. "Critical Notice: R. P. Henri Bernard, *Le Père Matthieu Ricci et la Société Chinoise de son temps* (1551–1610)." *Philobiblon*, No. 1 (June 1946):13–19.

C. S. Ch'ien. "Critical Notice: Kenneth Scott Latourette, *The Chinese: Their History and Culture*," *Philobiblon*, No. 2 (September 1946):30–37.

C. S. Ch'ien. "Critical Notice: Clara M. Candlin Young, *The Rapier of Lu, Patriot Poet of China.*" *Philobiblon,* No. 3 (December 1946):40–49.
The above three reviews are highly critical.
C. S. Ch'ien. "The Return of the Native." *Philobiblon,* No. 4 (March 1947):17–26.
"Shuo 'Hui Jia' " [Speaking of Returning Home]. *Guancha* II.1 (March 1947):24. Similar to the above.
"Bu Ping Yingwen Xin Cidian" [Supplementary Critique to the *New English Dictionary*]. *Guancha* III.5 (27 September 1947):21.
"Youlizhe de Yanjing" ([Review of] *The Traveller's Eye* [by Dorothy Carrington]). *Guancha* III.16 (13 December 1947):20.
"Xiaoshuo zhi Xiao" [Trivialities about Fiction]. *Xin Yu* (1947), pp. 22–24, 29–30. Light entertainment for the erudite.
"Zhongguo Shi yu Zhongguo Hua" [Chinese Poetry and Chinese Painting]. In *Kaiming Shudian Ershi Zhounian Wenji* [Literary Collection in Honor of the Twentieth Anniversary of the Kaiming Book Company]. Edited by Ma Xulun. Shanghai: Kaiming Shudian, 1947; Hong Kong: Longmen, 1969 (as single volume); also in *Qian Zhongshu Xuanji,* pp. 159–175, and *Jiu Wen Sipian.*
"Zayan" [Miscellany]. *Guancha* IV.2 (6 March 1948):18.
C. S. Ch'ien. "An Early Chinese Version of Longfellow's 'Psalm of Life.' " *Philobiblon* II.2 (No. 6) (March 1948):10–17. More on Sino-Western literary relations.
"Jingyin Ben *Tang Jihede* Yinyan" ([Translation of Heinrich Heine's] "Einleitung zur Prachtausgabe des *Don Quichotte*" [Introduction to the Splendid Edition of *Don Quixote*]). In *Wenxue Yanjiu Jikan* II. Peking: Renmin Wenxue Chubanshe, 1956, pp. 163–84. Qian notes on p. 184 that he had done an abridged translation in Paris in 1937, "while sojourning in Europe."
"*Han Changli Shi Xinian Jishi*" ([Review of] *Chronological Compendium of Notes on Han Changli's Poetry* [by Qian Zhonglian]). *Wenxue Yanjiu* 2 (1958):179–83. Qian was a member of the editorial board of this journal.
"Du 'Laaokong' " [Reading *Laocoon*]. *Wenxue Pinglun* 5 (1962):59–67. Also included in *Jiu Wen Sipian. Wenxue Yanjiu* changed its name to *Wenxue Pinglun* in 1959. Qian continued on the editorial board.
"Tonggan" [Synaesthesia]. *Wenxue Pinglun* 1 (1962):13–17. Also in *Jiu Wen Sipian.*

*"Lin Shu de Fanyi" [The Translations of Lin Shu]. In *Wenxue Yanjiu Jikan* I. Peking, 1964. I have not found this; the attribution is from *Renditions*, No. 5, p. 8.

"Classical Literary Scholarships in Modern China"/"Gudian Wenxue zai Xiandai Zhongguo." Peking, 1978. This bilingual pamphlet was produced for a sinological conference in Italy in 1978. The Chinese version has since been reprinted in *Ming Bao Yuekan* 165 (September 1979):37–38.

3. English Translations (by date of publication)

"The Besieged City" (Jeanne Kelly). *Renditions*, No. 2 (Spring 1974):65–80. Translation of the novel's first chapter.

"Lin Chin-nan Revisited" (George Kao). *Renditions*, No. 5 (Autumn 1975):8–21. A simplified translation of "Lin Shu de Fanyi" which leaves out the important section on *guwen* style.

Fortress Besieged (Jeanne Kelly and Nathan Mao). Bloomington: Indiana University Press, 1979. Complete translation of the novel with critical introduction and notes.

SECONDARY SOURCES

Bing Xi. "*Weng Cheng* Du Hou" [Having Read *Fortress Besieged*]. *Da Gong Bao*, 19 August 1947.

Fang Dan. "Wo suo Renshi de Qian Zhongshu" [The Qian Zhongshu I Know]. *Ming Bao Yuekan* 164 (August 1979):42–44.

Gunn, Edward M. *Unwelcome Muse: Chinese Literature in Shanghai and Peking*. New York: Columbia University Press, 1980. Pages 243–263 of this book concern Qian.

Hsia, C. T. See Xia Zhiqing.

Hu, Dennis T. "A Linguistic-Literary Approach to Ch'ien Chung-shu's Novel *Wei-ch'eng*." *Journal of Asian Studies* XXXVII.3 (May 1978):427–43. This study is part of a dissertation that appeared in 1977.

Lin Hai. "*Wei Cheng* yu *Tom Jones*" [*Wei Cheng* and *Tom Jones*]. *Guancha* V.14 (27 November 1948):12. Maintains Qian's work is a picaresque novel in the Fielding tradition.

*Murong Longtu. "Lun Qian Zhongshu de Xiaoshuo" [On Qian Zhongshu's Fiction]. *Pangu*, No. 37 (1971):26–31. Mentioned in Hu's article cited above.

Shui Jing. "Shi Qian [Paoshu] Zaji—Liang Wu Qian Zhongshu Xiansheng" [Notes on Attending Upon "Book-Thrower" Qian: Two Meetings with Mr. Qian Zhongshu]. *Ming Bao Yuekan* 163 (July 1979):35–41. Tries with something less than total success to capture the experience of meeting with Qian.

Wu Jiu. "Du *Wei Cheng*" [Reading *Wei Cheng*]. *Xiaoshuo Yuekan* I.1 (July 1948):90–95. Left-wing critique, voicing disappointment over the author's arrogance.

Xia Zhiqing [C. T. Hsia]. *A History of Modern Chinese Fiction.* New Haven: Yale University Press, 1971. 2nd ed. Has a chapter that is the first study on Qian in English.

———. "Zhuinian Qian Zhongshu Xiansheng" [Mourning Mr. Qian Zhongshu]. *Zhongguo Shibao* 9–10 February 1976.

———. "Chong Hui Qian Zhongshu Jishi" [Record of Meeting Qian Zhongshu Again]. *Zhongguo Shibao,* 16–17 June 1979.

Yan Jianbi. "[Review of] *Tan Yi Lu.*" *Yanjing Xuebao,* No. 35 (December 1948):271–83.

Zhang Yu. "Cong *Wei Cheng* Kan Qian Zhongshu" [Seeing through *Wei Cheng* to Qian Zhongshu]. *Tongdai Ren Wenyi Congkan* I.1 (20 April 1948). Similar to Wu Jiu's review, but more strident and *ad hominem.*

Zou Wenhai. "Yi Qian Zhongshu" [Remembering Qian Zhongshu]. *Zhuanji Wenxue* I.1 (June 1962):23–24.

Index

Airs of the States (*Guofeng banyuekan*), 4
Allegory, 66–67, 74, 156
Amis, Kingsley: *Lucky Jim*, 174n5
"Ancient-style" prose (*guwen*), 15–16, 18, 35–36, 43, 70
Archaism (*fugu*), 18, 59, 70
Aristotle, 66
Aurora Women's College, 7
Austen, Jane, 118

Ba Jin: *Cold Nights*, 9, 176n
Bagu wen. See "Eight-legged" essay
Bai Juyi, 31, 41, 50, 60
Babbitt, Irving, 3, 22
Bacon, Francis, 76, 77, 79, 84, 94
Baroque style (in prose), 73, 78, 128, 130
Baudelaire, Charles, 51
Blake, William, 20, 27
Bi ("familiar style"), 18
Bradley, A.C., 22
Buddhism, 34, 58, 62, 64, 99; on death, 28; influences on poets, 32
Burton, Robert, 73

Byron, Lord: *Vision of Judgement, The*, 104

Cao Baohua: *Odes to the Setting Sun*, 19–20, 22, 28, 39
"Capital Clique" (*Jing pai*), 111; compared with "Shanghai Clique" (*Hai pai*), 173n10
Chan [Buddhism], 28, 31; and poetry, 62, 64
Chedan fa ("nonsense" or "making light" method), 81, 82, 85, 97, 109, 114, 129, 130, 140, 151–52; defined, 79
Chen Yan, 4
Cheng Yi, 59
China Critic, 4
Chinese Academy of Sciences, 9, 34
Chinese Academy of Social Sciences, 11
Chinese Year Book (1944–45), 25
Chu Ci, 176n22
Ci. See Lyrics
Classic of Poetry, 11–12, 49
Ciceronian prose, 73
Confucius, 28, 46, 47, 49, 82, 167n28; *Confucian Analects*,

12, 53; Confucianism and literature, 14, 16, 40, 46, 59, 74; on death, 28; *Four Books*, 46; values of, 22, 70
Crescent Moon. See Xinyue Yuekan
Cultural Revolution, 10, 35

Da Dian, 58
Dante, Alighieri, 66, 87, 88; *Divine Comedy*, 87
Daoism, 28; and poetry, 34, 64
Dickens, Charles, 35
Didactic and expressive (theories of literature), *13–17*, 52, 93
Dream of the Red Chamber, 21, 26
Dryden, John: *Mac Flecknoe*, 104
Du Fu, 31, 39, 40, 41, 44, 50, 54
Du Mu, 50

"Eight-legged" essay *(bagu wen)*, 16, 43, 46, 71–72, 73, 80; "new" *bagu*, 76

Fang Bao, 35
Fei Ming, 77, 94
Feng Youlan, 3
Feng Zhi, 173n10
Fu. See Prose poetry
Fugu. See Archaism

Gauthier, Theophile, 50
Gongan school, *14–16*, 72, 74; Yuan brothers, 14
Gu Jiegang, 165–66n16
Guanghua University, 4
Guwen. See "Ancient-style" prose

Han Yu, 14, 15, 18, 31, 40, 44, 51, *57–60*, 61; and Buddhism, 58

Hardy, Thomas, 23; *Mayor of Casterbridge, The*, 128
He Jingming, 33
He Qifang, 9
Hebbel, Friedrich, 51
Hegel, G.W.F., 66; dialectical method of; 21, 156
Hu Shi, 71, 72, 73
Huang Tingjian, 31, 48
Huxley, Aldous, 5

Intelligentsia, 1–2, 10

Jiang Kui, 40
Jiang Yan, 57
Jiao Xun, *41–44*, 47
Jin Shengtan, 16, 34–35
Jindai Sanwen Chao, 17, 21

Lantian Normal College, 6–7
Lao She, 8
Le Gros Clark, C.D., 23, 40, 67
Lessing, G.E., 29, 34
Li Bo, 31, 55–56
Li He, 31, *48–57*, 58, 60, 61, 67
Li Shangyin, 14, 56
Li Yu, 16
Lin Shu, 3, 35–36
Lin Yutang, 114
Liu Dajie, 9
Liu Jiuyuan, 59
Liu Zongyuan, 14, 15
Lu Ji: *Wenfu*, 41
Lu Xun, 2, 17, 72, 74–76, 94; *"Jing Pai yu Hai Pai,"* 173n10; "Kong Yiji," 74–75; "On Fair Play," 75–76; "Lu

Xun style," 76; "Regret for the Past," 176n23
Lu You, 31
Luo Longji, 114
Luo Xianglin, 3
Lyrics *(Ci)*, 15, 32, 42–45

Malebranche, Nicolas de, 29
Mao Dun, 8, 9, 175n9, 176n23
Mao Zedong, 34
Martial, 92
Marxism, 10
May Fourth movement, 14, 17, 25, 68, 73, 74; generation of, 16; post-May Fourth period, 29, 48
Melville, Herman: *Confidence Man, The*, 136
Mencius, 46, 47
Meng Jiao, 31, 40
Metaphysical school (of Chinese poetry), 62
Montaigne, Michel de, 73, 94
Mysticism, 20, 28, 99

National Jinan University, 9
"Naive" and "sentimental" [poetry], 23, 25–26, 40–41
New Life movement, 98
Nietzsche, Friedrich, 164n13

Ouyang Xiu, 14
Oxford University, 4–5, 9, 24

Pan Dalin, 40
Pascal, Blaise, 74, 81
Philobiblon, 9, 28, 93
Poe, E.A., 51
Poetry *(shi)*, 15–16, 42–45, 47
Pope, Alexander: *Dunciad, The*, 104

Prose *(wen)*, 15, 18, 42–45; parallel prose, 43, 46; *xiaopin wen* ("familiar prose"), 17, 18
Prose-poetry *(fu)*, 23, 44
Proust, Marcel, 5

Qian Jibo, 2, 3, 4, 6
Qian Zhongshu: on literary genres, *42–45*, 46, 63; on literature and history, 33, 40, 47–48; mood frames in narrative, 103, 106, 110, 126–27, 154; on tradition, 29–30

WORKS: CRITICISM
Annotated Anthology of Song Poetry, *32–34*, 177–78
"Chinese Literature," *25–28*
"Chinese Poetry and Chinese Painting," *29–32*, 49
"Foreword" to *Prose Poetry of Su Tung-p'o, The, 23–24*, 40
History of Chinese Literature, 34
"On Lack of Obstruction," 178–79
Pipe-Awl Chapters, 11–12, 155
"Prolegomena to a Short History of Chinese Literature," 4, 178
"Reading *Laocoon*," *34–35*, 115
"Return of the Native," *28–29*, 93–94
"[Review of] *Jindai Sanwen Chao*," *17–19*, 21
"[Review of] *Luo Ri Song*," *19–21*, 22, 28, 39

"[Review of] *Zhongguo Xin Wenxue de Yuanliu,*" *13–17*, 19, 21, 25, 52, 71–72
"Synaesthesia," 34
Tan Yi Lu, 7, 8, 9, *37–39*, 70, 74, 100, 113, 155, 156, 159n18–22, 177
"Tragedy in Old Chinese Drama," *21–23*, 26
"Translations of Lin Shu, The," *35–36*, 181

WORKS: ESSAYS
"Discussing Friendship," *78–83*, 84, 85, 122
"Discussing Instruction," *84–93*
"Explaining Illiteracy," 171n25
"On Happiness," 171n28
"Prejudice, A," 170–71n23, 171n25
"Reading Aesop's Fables," 171n25
"Windows," 171n26
Written on the Margin of Life, 78, *83–95*, 103

WORKS: FICTION
"Cat, The," 105, *111–17*, 121
Fortress Besieged, 5, 6, 8, 9, 26, 95, 103, 105, 111, 117, *118–54*, 156–57, 159n22, 177; origin of name, 174n6
"God's Dream," *98–104*, 128, 144
Heart of the Artichoke, The, 8

Humans, Beasts and Ghosts, 8, *96–117*, 159n22, 177
"Inspiration," 97, *104–105*, 112
"Satan Pays an Evening Visit to Mr. Qian Zhongshu," 78, 96–98
"Souvenir," *105–10*

Qing (subjective feeling) and *jing* (outer reality), 129
Qinghua University, 3–4, 6, 9, 13; *Qinghua Zhoukan,* 4
Qu. *See* Song-poems
Qu Yuan, 50
Quarterly Bulletin of Chinese Bibliography, 24

"Reasoned exposition" *(daoli).* *See* "Sense of ideas"
Romance of the Three Kingdoms, 26
Ruan Yuan, 35
Rules of the Game, 115
Ruskin, John: "pathetic fallacy" of, 54

Saint John's University, 3
Sanwen ([plain] prose), 15
Schiller, Friedrich, 23, 40
Scholars, The, 35
"Sense of ideas *(liqu),* defined, 64, 67, 103; as opposed to "reasoned exposition" *(daoli),* 64–65, 100
Shakespeare, William; *Hamlet,* 92
Shaw, G.B., 90–91
Shen Congwen, 113
Shen Qiwu, 17, 21
Shi. See Poetry

Shi Tuo, 7, 9; *Marriage,* 9, 175n9
Shihua ("causeries on poetry"), 23, 37, 52, 57, 60–61
Shishuo Xinyu, 62
Sikong Tu, 62, 63; *Shi Pin,* 41, 67
Simile and Metaphor, 19–20, 28, 42, 93–94
Sitwell, Osbert, 161n12
Social Darwinism, 47, 98–99
Song-poems *(qu),* 15, 42–45, 46
Southwest Associated University, 6
Spinoza, Benedict de, 22
Spring and Autumn Annals, 49
Su Dongpo, 18, 23, 31, 51
Su Manshu, 52
Sun Yat-sen, 160n5

Tang Tao, 94
Tao Qian, 58
T'ien Hsia Monthly, 21, 26
Tongcheng school, 16, 35–36, 70

Vernacular language, 71–77, 93–95

Waley, Arthur, 60
Wang Anshi, 59
Wang Guowei, 21, 27, 44, 178–79
Wang Li, 94
Wang Shizhen (1526–1590), 41
Wang Shizhen (1634–1711), 62

Wang Wei, 31, 64
Waugh, Evelyn, 5, 156
Wen. See Prose
Wen Tingyun, 31
Wenxue Yanjiu, 32, 180
Wenxue Zazhi, 78
Wenyi Fuxing, 8
Wotton, Henry, 81
Wu Daoxuan, 31
Wu Mi, 3–4
Wu Shichang, 169n15

Xinyue Yuekan, 2, 4, 13, 17, 38
Xu Zhenqing, 39

Yan Yu, 62–63
Yang Jiang, 4, 5, 7, 8, 10
Yanghu and *Yangzhou* schools, 43
Ye Gongchao, 6
Yu Pingbo, 9
Yuan Mei: *Suiyuan Shihua,* 60–64
Yuan Zhen, 50

Zhang Ailing, 7
Zhang Ji, 58
Zhang Xuecheng, 17
Zhao Jingshen, 2, 13
Zhou Yang, 10
Zhou Zuoren, *13–16,* 19, 21, 25, 30, 52, 71–72, 73, 114
Zhu Guangqian, 78
Zhu Xi, 59
Zhu Ziqing, 3
Zou Wenhai, 2, 3